JN086576

日英対訳

英語で話す
世界情勢

山久瀬洋二 =著

IBCパブリッシング

装幀：岩目地英樹（コムデザイン）
翻訳・編集協力：Cristinee Bautista
　　　　　　　エド・ジェイコブ
　　　　　　　株式会社オフィス LEPS

［はじめに］
国際社会で話をするために

　この書籍では今世界で話題になり、さらに影響を与えている課題について、単にニュース的な解説と報道を紹介するのではなく、様々な角度から光を当て、課題の向こう側にある我々人類の課題や未来へのテーマに光を当てています。

　日本人は海外の人と交流をするときに、よく話題がなく、会話が進まないことに苦労しているといいます。本書はバイリンガルでここに書かれている英語を通して、相手と話すときの話題となるヒントを与えています。

　次のことを考えてみてください。

　例えば、アメリカや欧米の多くは移民社会です。その国の中に、世界とのリンクをもった人々が入って社会で暮らしを共にしています。こうした国では国内の問題と同様に、世界とその国との関連で、多くの国際問題についての話題が飛び交います。ですから、少なくとも、今起きている世界の事象について概略だけでも理解し、それが一つの国だけではなく、複数の国々にどのような影響を与えるかを知っておく必要があります。

　今、世界は「分断」という課題を抱えています。貧富の差、教育格差、南北問題や人種間の分断に加え、最近問題になっているロシアや中国などの国々と欧米の国々との価値観の違いがそれにあたります。こうした価値観の違いが会話の参加者の間に出てくるかもしれません。そこに気づいた状況をよく把握することも大切です。「君はどう思う?」と聞かれたとき、日本の事例をもとに説明し、意見を加えることが安全です。

　いずれにしろ、自分の意見をもって、それを表明する力があることは海外での交流においてとても大切です。それができないと、あなた自身の「質」を疑われる可能性もあります。これらの話題を通して、日本での課題と比較しなが

3

ら、そこから自らの意見を語ることで、そうした話題の中に自分の立ち位置
と、しっかりとした感想を持った人間だということがアピールできるのです。
海外の人はあなたが思っている以上に、政治や経済問題について人と話しま
す。日本人はそうした話題を社会の中で避ける傾向があります。そんな文化の
違いを常に心得て、海外の人と向き合うことが大切です。日本に来た海外の人
が、「日本では環境に対してどんなアプローチをしているの？」などと聞くこ
とがあります。そんなとき、本書にある環境問題に関する記事を思い出しなが
ら、自らのことを語ればいいのです。

　最後に、この書籍には、世界を見舞う重要な課題に対して頻繁に使われる単
語や表現がたくさん含まれています。中には学校で習わないものの、海外での
新聞やテレビ討論などでよく使用される用語、表現が含まれています。こうし
た表現を理解し、会話で使用することで、より深みのある交流を楽しんでくだ
さい。よく日本人が英語を使うとき、こうした単語が出てこないことで、会話
に行き詰まることがあります。大切なことは、こうした単語を少しでも駆使で
きるようにすることでしょう。もし単語が浮かんでこなければ、相手からその
表現を引き出したり、別の言葉に置き換えたりするスキルも大切です。ただ、
これらの単語や表現は複雑でも困難なものでもありません。本書を通してこう
した表現に触れ、彼らが世界の課題に対してどのようなアプローチで会話をし
ているのか、ヒントを感じてもらえれば幸いです。

山久瀬 洋二

［はじめに］
国際社会で話をするために ……………………………………………3

第 1 章 ウクライナ問題と世界情勢 11
Chapter 1 The Ukraine Issue and the Global Situation

第 1 話　ロシアのウクライナ侵攻がもたらす脅威 ……………………13
Article 1　Underlying Factors and Threats Posed by the Russian Invasion
of Ukraine

第 2 話　ウクライナを支える若き指導者とハイテク技術……………21
Article 2　Young Leaders and Advanced Technology Supporting Ukraine

第 3 話　ロシアへの対応に苦慮する中国の本音 ……………………29
Article 3　China's True Intentions as It Struggles to Deal with Russia

第 4 話　ウクライナ問題の背景に見えるプロテスタンティズムの
ビジネス観……………………………………………………39
Article 4　Protestantism's View of Business in the Context of the Ukraine
Issue

第 5 話　ディアスポラと国際政治 ………………………………………49
Article 5　Diaspora and International Politics

第 2 章 アメリカ外交と民主主義　　59
Chapter 2 US Diplomacy and Democracy

第6話　波紋を呼んだ国際社会でのアメリカ大統領の発言 ⋯⋯⋯⋯⋯61
Article 6　Remarks by the President of the United States to the
International Community Cause Controversy

第7話　「是は是、非は非」が通らない複雑な2022年 ⋯⋯⋯⋯⋯⋯69
Article 7　A Complicated 2022 in Which "Right Is Right, Wrong Is Wrong"
Does Not Work

第8話　タリバンのアフガニスタン制圧がもたらす影響 ⋯⋯⋯⋯⋯77
Article 8　Impacts of the Taliban on Afghanistan and the World

第9話　深刻化する米中対立とネット世界 ⋯⋯⋯⋯⋯⋯⋯⋯⋯87
Article 9　The Ever-Growing US-China Feud and the Online World

第10話　ポピュリズムの政策に翻弄された世界の実情 ⋯⋯⋯⋯⋯95
Article 10　The Realities of a World at the Mercy of Populist Policies

第 3 章 複雑化・多様化する国際社会　　103
Chapter 3 An Increasingly Complex and Diverse
International Society

第11話　カリブ系のアーバンポップスが象徴するアメリカの世情 ⋯⋯ 105
Article 11　America as Symbolized by Caribbean Urban Pop Music

第12話　中東の文明へのプライドが生み出す欧米との確執 ⋯⋯⋯ 113
Article 12　Pride in Middle Eastern Civilization Sparks Feuds in the West

第13話　宗教と科学の課題を突きつけるインドのコロナ禍············ 121
Article 13　India's Covid Disaster Puts Religion and Science on the Line

第14話　フランス大統領選挙の結果から見るEUの行方 ··············· 129
Article 14　The Future of the European Union after the French Presidential
Elections

第15話　女王の死去から見えてくるイギリス王室の1000年の
レガシー ··· 139
Article 15　The Queen's Death Reveals the Thousand-Year Legacy
of the British Royal Family

第16話　極東情勢を左右する日韓の対立の長い歴史 ····················· 149
Article 16　The Long History of Conflict between Japan and South Korea
and Its Effects on the Far East

第 4 章　世界経済の未来　　159
Chapter 4　The Future of the Global Economy

第17話　世界経済の覇者を決める電気自動車····························· 161
Article 17　Electric Vehicles Decide Who Will Dominate the World Economy

第18話　テスラはAIで次世代に挑戦する ······························· 169
Article 18　Tesla Challenges the Next Generation with AI

第19話　セミコンダクターの不足を鳥瞰すれば························· 177
Article 19　A Bird's-Eye View of the Semiconductor Shortage

第20話　ナリウッドに象徴されるグローバルな人材交流··············· 185
Article 20　Global Talent Exchange Symbolized by Nollywood and Others

第 5 章 世界から見た日本 193
Chapter 5 Japan from a Global Perspective

第21話　安倍元首相銃撃事件から見える日本人の意識 ················· 195
Article 21　Japanese Attitudes Seen in the Shooting of Former
　　　　　 Prime Minister Abe

第22話　ゴッホとイーロン・マスク
　　　　 ──2人から見たイノベーションの本質 ························· 203
Article 22　Van Gogh and Elon Musk—The Essence of Innovation
　　　　　 from Their Point of View

第23話　「日本人の心」を静かにアピールしたキャディの一礼 ······· 211
Article 23　The Quiet Appeal of the "Japanese Spirit" in
　　　　　 a Caddie's Bow

第24話　世界にとって新鮮な「受け入れる」という発想 ················· 219
Article 24　A Fresh Idea of "Acceptance" for the World

第 6 章 世界、そして未来への課題 229
Chapter 6 Challenges for the World and the Future

第25話　格差社会に影響を与える地球温暖化 ···························· 231
Article 25　Global Warming Affecting Disparities

第26話　南北問題と民主主義の確執に揺れるノーベル賞 ············· 239
Article 26　Nobel Prize Shaken by North-South Problem and Democracy
　　　　　 Feuds

第27話　政治とスポーツ、そして芸術との関係とは……………………… 247
Article 27　What Is the Relationship between Politics, Sports, and the Arts?

第28話　文明の磁場の逆転が進む中で迷走するアジアとアメリカ…255
Article 28　Asia and America Lost in the Progressive Reversal of
　　　　　　Civilization's Magnetic Field

第29話　人種や宗教の対立を乗り越えるには………………………… 263
Article 29　Overcoming Racial and Religious Conflicts

エピローグ　世代を超えた人類の葛藤と闘いの　　　271
　　　　　その先へ
Epilogue　Beyond the Conflicts and Struggles of Mankind
　　　　　across Generations

最 終 話　犠牲を乗り越えた人類の長い道のり …………………………… 273
Last Article　The Long Road to Humanity Overcoming Sacrifice

第1章

ウクライナ問題と世界情勢

Chapter 1

The Ukraine Issue and the Global Situation

第1話
ロシアのウクライナ侵攻がもたらす脅威

Article 1
Underlying Factors and Threats Posed
by the Russian Invasion of Ukraine

Facing a building threat from Russia, Ukraine's president sought security guarantees from NATO's chief in a meeting on Thursday and came away with a renewed commitment that his country could eventually join the military alliance despite stiff objections from its Russian neighbors.

—— New York Times

（ロシアの脅威に直面しているウクライナの大統領は、木曜日の会合でNATOの首脳に安全保障を求め、近隣のロシアからの強い反対にもかかわらず、最終的に軍事同盟に加盟することを改めて約束した）

Russian forces have invaded Ukraine, exerting pressure on and threatening not only it but Western Europe as well. The **atrocities** committed by Russian forces on the Ukrainian battlefield have shocked the world.

The reason for Russia's invasion, however, was that it saw Belarus and Ukraine as the front lines in defending its own **interests** from the threat of the West. Based on an alliance with Belarus, it invaded Ukraine's borders from the north and east simultaneously.

This sudden invasion created a state of emergency for NATO (The North Atlantic Treaty Organization) and the US. There has even been speculation that China, after carefully **assessing** the situation and the extent of its influence, might choose to pursue plans to invade Taiwan, over which it claims **sovereignty**. The two great powers of Russia and the US, both possessing nuclear weapons, continue to attempt to keep each other in check, creating tensions that could possibly provoke a third world war.

Since the 19th century or even earlier, Eastern Europe has been a mixture of diverse ethnic groups and has always been called the **powder keg** of the European region. The background is complex, but to further highlight an important point, similar **ethnic** and international problems are spreading throughout the world, including Asia, where they are intermingled and ignited.

In the Donbass region of eastern Ukraine, where fierce fighting continues, Russian residents originally made up the **majority** of the population. They speak Russian and many are eager to possess Russian passports. The rest of the country, on the other hand, is inhabited by people of Ukrainian ancestry, many of whom are descendants of those who originally immigrated

▶ invade → p.20

ウクライナにロシア軍が**侵攻**し、ウクライナのみならず西欧に圧力と脅威を与えています。ウクライナの戦場で明らかになるロシア軍による**残虐行為**には目を覆いたくなるものがあります。

ロシアは、ベラルーシとウクライナはどちらも西側と国境を接した自国の**権益**を守る最前線と意識していました。そんなベラルーシとの同盟をもとに、ウクライナの北側から、そして東側から一挙に国境を侵犯したのです。

ロシアのウクライナ侵攻によって、アメリカを含むNATOは緊急事態となりました。その様子と影響力の大きさを慎重に**見極めた**上で、中国が自らの**主権**を主張する台湾への侵攻を計画するのではないかという憶測も流れました。核を持つ大国同士がお互いを牽制しながら、世界大戦すれすれの緊張を生み出しているのです。

▶ NATO（北大西洋条約機構）は北米2か国と欧州28か国の計30か国が加盟する政府間軍事同盟。本部はベルギーのブリュッセル。日本は「グローバル・パートナー国」として協力関係を構築している。

そもそも19世紀、あるいはそれ以前から、東欧は多様な民族が入り乱れ、常にヨーロッパ地域の**火薬庫**と言われてきました。その背景は複雑です。しかしさらに強調すれば、同様の**民族**問題と国際問題が交錯して火種となっている地域はアジアを含め世界中に拡散しています。

今、激しい戦闘が続いているウクライナ東部のドンバス地方は、元々ロシア系の住民が**多数派**として居住する地域です。彼らはロシア語を話し、多くはロシア国籍のパスポートを持つことを希望しています。一方、それ以外の地域はウクライナ系の人が居住しますが、元々ポーランドが強国だった頃に移住してきた人々の子孫も多く

from Poland when it was a mighty nation.

Ukraine has been always rich in natural and agricultural resources, which is why nearby powerful countries have long eyed its wealth. However, after the former Russian Empire eliminated influence from Poland and other neighboring nations, Ukraine became Russian territory and it only gained independence after World War I.

However, Ukraine was later swept away by **socialist movements** and became a republic annexed by the Soviet Union. At that time, the Crimean Peninsula, facing the Black Sea, and the previously mentioned Donbass region with its substantial Russian population also became parts of Ukraine. Many Ukrainians were purged or forcibly displaced under the influence of the power politics of Stalin's regime, which resulted in huge numbers of casualties. For this reason, anti-Soviet sentiments grew, and when World War II began and the Soviet Union and Germany went to war, some people of Ukrainian descent cooperated with the Nazis.

These complicated circumstances remained significant when the Soviet Union collapsed in the 1980s and Ukraine once more became independent with the **borders** set by the former Soviet Union. Russia's attempt to boost its national power under President Vladimir Putin led to the problems we are witnessing today. First, in 2014, Russian troops invaded the Crimean Peninsula, separating it from Ukraine and making it Russian territory. This was possible due to the **overwhelming support** of the Russian people and heightened President Putin's **approval ratings**. In response, the Russian residents of eastern Ukraine began to riot, demanding that the area belonged to Russia. This marked the beginning of the turmoil that continues to this day. In the midst of these threats, President Zelensky, a former

います。

　ウクライナは天然資源と農業資源に恵まれたところでもあり、近隣の強国は常にその富に関心を持ってきました。特に旧ロシア帝国がポーランドなどの周辺国の影響を排除したのちは、ウクライナはロシア領となり第一次世界大戦を経てやっと独立できたのです。

　しかし、ウクライナはその後**社会主義運動**の波に飲み込まれ、ソ連に併合された共和国となりました。その折に黒海に面したクリミア半島や、ロシア系住民の多く住むドンバス地方もウクライナとなりました。ウクライナ人はスターリン政権下の強権政治の影響で有力者の粛清や強制移住などを経験するなかで、多数の犠牲者を出しました。そのために、反ソ連意識が高まり、第二次世界大戦が始まってソ連とドイツが開戦すると、ウクライナ系の人々の中にはナチスに協力する人もいたのです。

　こうした複雑な事情を抱えたまま、1980年代にソ連が崩壊し、ウクライナが再び旧ソ連の設定した**国境**のまま独立したのです。そして、ロシアが次第にプーチン大統領のもとで国力を蓄えたことが、今回の問題の原因となりました。まず、2014年にクリミア半島にロシア軍が侵攻し、ウクライナから切り離しロシア領とします。これはロシア国民の**圧倒的な支持**のもとに行われ、プーチン大統領の**支持率上昇**の後押しにもなりました。そして、それに呼応するようにウクライナ東部のロシア系住民がロシアへの帰属を求めて騒乱を起こしたのです。2014年から現在に至る混乱の始まりです。そうした脅威の中で、以前はウクライナのテレビ番組でコメディアンとして人気を博していたゼレンスキー大統領が、政権の腐敗を**根絶**

comedian on Ukrainian television, actively sought to introduce democracy as a means of **eradicating** corruption in the regime and suggested joining NATO and the EU, which provoked Russia.

Conversely, Americans comment that the situation is similar to that of the US in the 1960s. When a revolution took place in Cuba, a country very close to the US, and a more Soviet-leaning government was formed, the US felt as if a knife were being held to its throat and pursued a **hardline policy**. Ukraine is a neighbor of Russia with a vast territory, so when Ukraine announced it would join NATO, Russia considered the move to be a significant threat because it viewed Ukraine and Belarus as **satellite states**.

The issue of how different ethnic and racial groups can co-exist in harmony within a nation is the most important theme that modern society must overcome. And this incident shows us that when the surrounding powers **intervene** in such situations, it will greatly affect the future of not only the region but also the world.

するために民主主義を積極的に導入しようとし、NATO
やEUへの加盟を示唆したことでロシアを刺激したので
す。

　これに対して、アメリカ人は、この状況は60年代の
アメリカにそっくりだとコメントします。アメリカのす
ぐそばにあるキューバに革命が起こり、ソ連寄りの政権
ができたとき、アメリカは喉元にナイフを突きつけられ
たと思い、**強硬な政策**をとり続けました。ウクライナは
広大な土地を持つロシアの隣国です。そのウクライナが
NATOに加盟すると表明したことが、元々ウクライナと
ベラルーシをロシアの**衛星国家**であると意識していたロ
シアにとっては大きな脅威となったわけです。

　一つの国家の中で異なる民族や人種がいかに融和し、
共存してゆくかという課題は、現代社会が乗り越えなけ
ればならない最も重要なテーマです。そして、このテー
マに周囲の大国が**介入**したとき、その地域だけではなく、
世界の未来をも大きく左右してしまうことを、今回の事
件は我々に示しているのです。

ウクライナと周辺国

INVADE 侵攻する、侵略する

　征服や占領のために「軍事力によって他国や他の領域に攻め入る」ことを表します。海外メディアがロシアによるウクライナへの侵攻を伝える際、名詞のinvasionとともによく使われています。また、同様に使われているのがaggressionという名詞で、「侵略」や「他国への攻撃、武力行使」という意味です。海外の政府機関やマスメディアがどのような言葉を使用しているのか注目してみると、世界情勢を理解し、さらに自分の意見を語るうえで役に立つ語彙を増やすことができるでしょう。

　invadeやinvasionは他にも「〔病原菌やウイルスなどが〕侵入する・まん延する」ことや、「〔権利などを〕侵害する」ことも意味します。

⸺⸺⸺⸺⸺⸺⸺⸺⸺⸺⸺⸺⸺⸺⸺⸺

例文

The Soviet Union invaded Afghanistan in December 1979.
ソ連は1979年12月にアフガニスタンに侵攻した。

It is nothing less than an invasion of privacy.
それはプライバシーの侵害に他ならない。

We have to defend our country from the foreign aggression.
我々は外国の侵略から国を守らなくてはならない。

❓ あなたはどう答える？

If a foreign country invaded Japan's territory, how should Japan respond?
外国が日本の領土を侵犯してきたら、日本はどのように対処するのですか？

ヒント ▶ 日本は島国なので陸続きに接する国はありませんが、海を挟んで韓国・北朝鮮、中国、ロシア、フィリピンなどが近くにあります。在日米軍はアジア有事の際の重要拠点です。

覚えておくと便利な単語、表現

☐ **based on an alliance with** 〜との同盟に基づいて
☐ **border** 〔〜に〕隣接する
☐ **keep [hold] ~ in check** 〜をけん制する

第2話
ウクライナを支える若き指導者と
ハイテク技術

Article 2
Young Leaders and Advanced Technology
Supporting Ukraine

Ukraine has started using Clearview AI's facial recognition during war

—— Reuters

（ウクライナは戦争にあたり、クリアビュー AI の顔認識システムの使用を開始した）

When Russian troops invaded Ukraine, it was Tesla **founder** Elon Musk who was the first to **announce** his support for the war-stricken country. He provided Ukraine with Starlink devices, which were used to prevent the Russians from cutting Ukraine off from the internet. These satellite-controlled devices basically provided a network that enabled internet communication in any location.

In 2019, a 28-year-old man was selected as **deputy prime minister** of Ukraine. Mykhailo Fedorov was responsible for digital reforms in Ukraine's public institutions. To his credit, Ukraine became the first country in the world to issue electronic passports, and many **government services** can now be enjoyed instantly online. Speedy, paperless service has become available in all parts of the country. Even more interesting is a system called E-Residency, which allows foreign nationals to access Ukrainian administrative services online in order to do business in the country. When the Russian military invasion was confirmed, Mr. Fedorov used Twitter to ask Elon Musk for **assistance** in dealing with the Russian cyberattack. Musk gave the go signal in just one hour, and the decision was made to provide Starlink.

Fedorov has also called on hackers from around the world to interfere with communications in Russia. Hackers are often mistakenly thought of as cyberterrorists who flood computer networks

　ウクライナにロシア軍が侵攻してきたとき、真っ先に
ウクライナへの支援を**表明**したのが、テスラの**創業者**イ
ーロン・マスク氏です。彼がスターリンクの端末をウク
ライナに提供し、ロシア側がウクライナのネット環境に
ダメージを与えることを妨害したのです。衛星からどの
ような場所にも通信環境を提供できるネットワークが供
与されたわけです。

イーロン・マスク

　ウクライナでは、2019年に一人の青年が**副首相**に抜
擢されました。当時まだ28歳だったミハエロ・フェド
ロフ氏が副首相となり担ったのが、ウクライナの公的機
関でのデジタル改革でした。彼の功績で、ウクライナは
世界でも初めての電子パスポートを発行し、**行政サー
ビス**の多くもオンラインで瞬時に享受できるようになり
ました。国内各地でペーパーレス化と迅速なサービスが
受けられるようになったわけです。さらに興味深いのが
e-Residencyと呼ばれる、外国籍の人がオンラインで
ウクライナ国内の行政サービスにアクセスでき、ウクラ
イナ国内でビジネスができるシステムを構築したことで
す。そのフェドロフ氏がロシア軍の侵攻が確認されたと
き、イーロン・マスク氏にTwitterでロシアのサイバー
攻撃への対応について**援助**を求めたのです。マスク氏は
その呼びかけにたった1時間でゴーサインを出して、ス
ターリンクの供与が決まりました。

　さらにフェドロフ氏は、世界中のハッカーに呼びかけ、
ロシアに通信障害が起きるように手配します。ハッカー
といえば、我々はコンピュータネットワークにウイルス
を流し込むようなサイバーテロリストだと誤解しがちで
すが、ハッカーの多くはホワイトハッカーと呼ばれ、そ
うしたサイバー攻撃を防いだり、テロリストを追いつめ

with viruses, but many are white hat hackers, who are important in preventing cyberattacks and tracking down terrorists. That is why Deputy Prime Minister Fedorov has gathered hackers to participate in **combat operations** in virtual space.

As the Russians were closing in on Kyiv, the following technique was introduced to further contain Russian troop movements: Fedorov contacted Hoan Ton-That, a Vietnamese-Australian currently residing in New York City who operates a cutting-edge tech company called Clearview AI. It uses a system that **recognizes** and identifies human faces based on a huge database. This database is used by government agencies to maintain **public safety**.

Clearview AI's technology has now enabled the Ukrainian side to identify the faces of Russian soldiers at checkpoints, thereby preventing sabotage by the Russian military. This system can also be used to reunite families separated by war. The precision of this technology is so impressive that it can even identify dead war casualties whose faces have been mutilated, so it is especially useful in providing accurate information on the Russian military's casualties.

たりする重要な人材です。フェドロフ副首相は、バーチャル空間での**戦闘行為**に参加してもらうためにハッカーを組織化したわけです。

そして、ロシア軍がキーウに迫っていた頃、ロシア軍の動きをさらに封じるための次の技術が導入されました。彼は、ベトナム系オーストラリア人で、現在ニューヨークに居を構えるホアン・トンタット氏と連絡を取ったのです。ホアン・トンタット氏が運営するクリアビュー AIという会社は、膨大なデータベースをもとに人の顔を**認識し**特定するシステムを持つ先端企業です。この会社のデータベースは行政機関の**治安維持**などに使用されてきました。

しかし、今回クリアビュー AIの技術によって、ウクライナ側はロシア軍兵士の顔を識別でき、検問所では顔を識別することで、ロシア軍の動きを鈍化させることも可能になりました。戦争で離散した家族の再会のためにも、このシステムは活用できます。なんと、戦死者の損傷した顔からもその人物が特定できるほどに精密な技術のため、ロシア軍の戦死者の情報も的確に把握できるのだというから驚かされます。

Today in the cyber world, various **talents** are scattered among various countries. The Philippines and Vietnam, in particular, are said to be treasure troves of such talent, with Hoan Ton-That as living proof of this.

And it is because of this young deputy prime minister that the Ukrainian military, **contrary to initial predictions**, has been able to resist the Russian threat and to immediately publicize concrete evidence of Russian **war crimes** in the occupied territories.

It is also important to recognize the advantages of President Zelensky's decision to appoint a man in his 20s as deputy prime minister, as well as Zelensky's flexible and **resourceful** response to push for digital reforms. Ukraine, which was said to be **considerably weaker** than Russia at the beginning of the war, has been able to stubbornly resist because of the president's use of the latest media and internet technology to call on the world to unite with him.

As society is quickly adjusting to online information and the development of AI, there is also a growing risk to people's online security. New technology provides **authorities** more power to access and possibly abuse personal information. However, we can always come up with ways of overcoming these security breaches through cybersecurity technology. The fact that **groups of brilliant minds** in unexpected places, such as the Philippines, Vietnam, the Baltic States, and Ukraine, have been so active and have made significant contributions to the defense of Ukraine in the current war may have provided us a very useful hint about future solutions to the many controversial issues our internet society is facing.

▶ authority → p.28

　現在、サイバーの世界では様々な**才能**が世界各地に点在しています。特にフィリピンやベトナムなどはそうした人材の宝庫と言われており、ホアン・トンタット氏はその証の一人といえるでしょう。

　そして、ウクライナ軍が**当初の予測に反して**頑強にロシアの脅威に抵抗でき、ロシア軍の占領地での**戦争犯罪**行為に対しても具体的な証拠を即座に公にできるのは、この若き副首相の存在があるからなのです。

　20代の人物を副首相に抜擢し、デジタル改革を押し進めるような柔軟で**臨機応変な**対応をしたゼレンスキー大統領の英断にも注目する必要があります。戦争が始まった当初から、**圧倒的に劣勢**だと言われたウクライナが頑強に抵抗できるのも、大統領が最新のメディアやネット技術を駆使して、世界に団結を呼びかけたからに他なりません。

　もちろん、AI化や情報のオンライン化には、個人情報の問題や**権力**による乱用の問題が付きまといます。しかし、仮にそうした問題があったにせよ、サイバーセキュリティの技術を駆使してその課題を乗り越えるノウハウの追求もしなければなりません。そんな**頭脳集団**が、フィリピンやベトナム、あるいはバルト三国やウクライナといったような、思わぬところで活動をし、今回の戦争でもウクライナの防衛に大きく貢献したことは、議論の多いネット社会の未来に一つの明るいヒントを与えたのかもしれません。

Key word

AUTHORITY　権力、権威

　第一義として「法の執行や命令を下すことができる力や権利」を表しますが、そうした力を委任された「権力者、支配者」や「〔行政権がある〕機関、官公庁」のことも表します。本文では個人情報を提供される、または乱用する対象として使われているので後者の意味で解釈するとよいでしょう。

　同じ「権力」という意味ではpowerという単語も使用されますが、こちらはどちらかというと能力や実力によって得られる権威、権限を表します。authorityは公的に認められた、あるいは地位や立場によって与えられる権威、権限ということを意味します。

....

例文

In Japan, there is also a risk of abuse of personal information by the authorities.
日本でも個人情報が権力によって乱用されるリスクがある。

The authorities managed to stabilize the currency.
当局が自国の通貨をなんとか安定させた。

He gained his power through hard work.
彼は努力によって権力を得た。

？　あなたはどう答える？

What are the advantages and problems of moving Japanese administrative services online?
日本の行政サービスのオンライン化にはどのような利点と問題点がありますか？

> **ヒント**　日本は行政手続の原則オンライン化を目指していますが、その利用率は先進国の中でも最低レベルです。添付書類や本人確認が必要になることで利用率が下がるようです。

覚えておくと便利な単語、表現

☐ **abuse personal information**　個人情報を乱用する

☐ **access ~ online**　オンラインで〜にアクセスする

☐ **speedy and paperless procedure**　迅速かつペーパーレスな手続き

第3話
ロシアへの対応に苦慮する中国の本音

Article 3
China's True Intentions as It Struggles to Deal with Russia

Biden expected to urge China not to offer Russia any help

—— BBC

（バイデン大統領は中国がロシアにどんな援助も行わないよう説得した模様）

The scene on the way from Ninoy Aquino International Airport in Manila, the capital of the Philippines, to the city's downtown offers one **clue** to a world shaken by the Russian military invasion of Ukraine. It shows China's **expansion** into Asia. During the last two years of the global coronavirus epidemic, Chinese capital has clearly accelerated its expansion into Asia.

In Pasay, an area on the way to downtown, there is an industrial commercial district centered around a large shopping mall called the SM Mall of Asia.

In one corner of this area, a new Chinatown has been established in the past two years. Of course, it is not the stereotypical "Chinatown" we imagine, but a modern **commercial complex** lined with restaurants and entertainment venues, the scale of which is astonishing.

In Cebu, another economic hub of the Philippines, a large-scale **Chinese-funded** business center is being built on the east coast, on Mactan Island, where the international airport is located. Similar developments seem to be happening all over Asia.

And there is another major power in Asia.

That is India. Japan has been working to strengthen its relationship with India to guard against and check China's advance into Asia. As a result, Japan created a system called QUAD, which strengthens security and economic cooperation with India, Australia, and the US.

However, India is faced with a complicated situation. It originally had **border issues** with China and has always **been very wary** of its expansion. That is also the reason India joined QUAD. However, India has also maintained close ties with Russia, partly because of China's conflict with the former Soviet

► expansion → p.38

　フィリピンの首都マニラのニノイ・アキノ国際空港から、市のダウンタウンに向かう途中の光景には、ウクライナへのロシア軍の侵攻で揺れる世界を考える、一つの**ヒント**があります。それは中国のアジアへの**進出**です。コロナウイルスが世界で流行したこの2年の間に、中国資本は明らかにアジア進出を加速しています。

　ダウンタウンへの途上にあるパサイという地区には、モール・オブ・アジアという大型のショッピングモールを中心とした産業商業地区があります。

　その一角に、この2年の間に新たなチャイナタウンができ上がっています。もちろん我々がイメージするステレオタイプな「中華街」ではなく、モダンな**複合商業施設**にレストランやエンターテインメント施設が並んでおり、その規模には驚かされます。

　フィリピン経済のもう一つのハブであるセブでも、セブ島の東海岸、国際空港のあるマクタン島に、**中国資本による**大規模なビジネスセンターが建設されています。同様の動きはアジアのあちこちで起こっているはずです。

　そして、アジアにはもう一つの大国があります。

　それはインドです。日本は中国のアジア進出に対する警戒と牽制のために、インドとの関係強化に努めてきました。その結果、日本はQUAD（クアッド）と呼ばれるインド、オーストラリアにアメリカを絡めた安全保障と経済協力関係を強化する仕組みをつくりました。

　しかし、インドは複雑な状況に追い込まれています。インドは元々、中国と**国境問題**を抱えていて、中国の進出には常に**強い警戒感を持って**いました。それがQUADに参加した理由でもあります。ただ、インドは中国が旧ソ連と対立していたこともあって、ロシアとも深いパイプ

▶QUAD（4か国戦略対話）は戦略的同盟を結んでいる日米豪印の4か国における会談。自由や民主主義といった基本的価値を共有する4か国の枠組みとしているが、実質は対中包囲網だという解釈が広くみられる。

31

Union. Since Russia invaded Ukraine, India has maintained an **ambivalent** attitude toward it. Due in part to political problems with Pakistan, India's arch-enemy, India's traditional policy has been to maintain ties with Russia while keeping China in check.

This ambiguous response by India could, of course, put a crack in the QUAD alliance.

Let us return again to China. With Russia's invasion of Ukraine, everyone was concerned about what China would do. However, China cannot hide its **bewilderment** at Russia's actions. China, which was originally trying to work with Russia to counter the US, has found itself in a **predicament** that it cannot cope with.

In order to link its economic advances in Asia to the European **economic bloc**, China was planning to expand its economy from the former Eastern European bloc into Africa as well. This is the so-called "Belt and Road Initiative." In fact, Ukraine was also a key point in that strategy.

を維持してきたのです。ロシアがウクライナに侵攻して以来、インドはロシアに対して**曖昧な**態度を続けています。インドの仇敵パキスタンとの政治問題もあり、中国を牽制しながらロシアとは紐帯を、というのが伝統的なインドの方針だったのです。

インドのこの曖昧な対応は、当然QUADでの同盟にヒビを入れる可能性もあります。

再び中国に話を戻しましょう。ロシアのウクライナ侵攻で誰もが気にしたのは、中国の動きです。しかし、中国はロシアの動きに**戸惑い**を隠せません。元々ロシアと連携してアメリカに対抗しようとしていた中国が、対応できないような**苦境**に陥ってしまったのです。

中国はアジアに向けた経済進出をヨーロッパ**経済圏**へと繋いでゆくために、旧東欧圏からアフリカへもリンクする経済進出を企画していました。それが「一帯一路」と呼ばれる戦略です。実は、ウクライナはその戦略の重要なポイントでもありました。

▶一帯一路は中国が推進するアジア・中東・欧州・アフリカにわたる広域経済圏の構想。中国から欧州までつながる陸路と東南アジア・南アジア・中東・アフリカを結ぶ海路の地域で、インフラ整備や資金の往来を促進する。

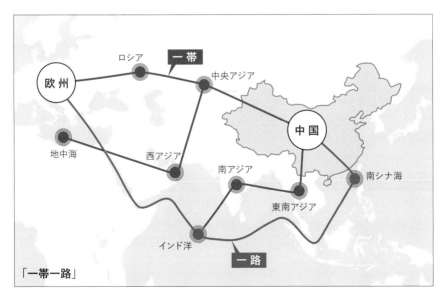

「一帯一路」

However, Russia launched an invasion of Ukraine. Moreover, this united not only the Western community but also most of the international community. This is why China cannot actively defend Russia's actions. Moreover, following the **suppression** of democracy in Hong Kong, China, which has been seeking to integrate Taiwan, has become unsure about the timing for doing so.

Thus, the crisis in Ukraine has had a major impact on the policies of the two Asian powers.

If one simply considers China's economic advance in the Philippines, its movements up until Russia's invasion of Ukraine were clearly intended to keep the US in check, aiming for **hegemony** in Asia. However, when Russia invaded, China, which could reasonably have been expected to immediately join Russia, responded slowly, showing how much pressure China is under from the international community. If China supports Russia's unexpected move this time, there is a possibility that there will be a **backlash** from China's friends who expected benefits from the "One Belt, One Road" plan. That said, Russia must desperately want China's support. However, China cannot easily accept such an invitation. This contradiction plagues China.

The same is true for India. India has traditionally been wary of American expansion into Asia, hiding within its society a **feud** between South India, which is more deeply influenced by Hinduism, and North India, where the influence of Islamic society remains. India was strongly aware of China, and immediately after it joined hands with the US via Japan and Australia, Russia, a friendly country, **went on a rampage**.

In the Philippines, the Ukraine issue seems distant, as if unrelated to these international feuds. Perhaps due in part to

　ところが、ロシアがそのウクライナに侵攻を始めたのです。しかも、そのことによって西欧社会のみならず、ほとんどの国際社会が結束してしまいました。これが、中国がロシアの行動を積極的に擁護できない理由です。しかも、香港での民主化の弾圧に次いで、台湾統合を模索していた中国は、そのタイミングも見えなくなりました。

　このように、ウクライナの危機はアジアの二つの大国の方針に大きな影響を与えました。

　フィリピンで見られる中国の経済進出を単純に考えれば、ロシアのウクライナ侵攻前までの中国の動きは、アジアでの覇権を狙いアメリカを牽制する明快なものでした。しかし、ロシアが侵攻したとき、合理的に考えれば即座にロシア側につきそうな中国の動きが鈍くなったことは、国際社会の圧力の下で中国がいかに困っているかを物語っています。今回のロシアの思わぬ動きをもし中国が支持すれば、「一帯一路」の恩恵を期待していた中国の友好国の反発を受ける可能性もあります。とはいえ、ロシアは中国の支持が喉から手が出るほど欲しいはずです。しかし、中国はその誘いには安易に乗れません。この矛盾が中国を悩ませているのです。

　インドにとってもそれは同様です。インドはより深くヒンドゥー教の影響のある南インドと、イスラム社会の影響が残る北インドとの確執を社会の中に隠しながら、伝統的にアメリカのアジア進出には警戒感を持っていました。そのインドが中国を意識して、日本とオーストラリアを経てアメリカと手を結んだ直後に友好国のロシアが暴挙に出たわけです。

　フィリピンでは、こうした国際社会の確執とは無縁のように、ウクライナ問題が遠くに見えてしまいます。中

China's expansion, rather than economic damage from the coronavirus pandemic, the city even seems more vibrant than ever, and infrastructure work is steadily progressing to relieve Manila's daunting **traffic congestion**.

The sanctions against Russia may deal a new **economic blow** to these promising countries. If this is the case, it may be in China's best interest to avoid creating overt conflict with major Western countries and to quietly continue to provide economic enrichment to these regions. China should be asking itself about the merits of its decision.

Just like in the headlines, news broke that President Biden had warned Chinese President Xi Jinping not to aid Russia during a telephone conversation. The important thing to remember, however, is that while considering the delicate situation in China, it may be in our best interest as a strategy against Russia to quietly watch the situation so as not to push it over the edge. But this is the kind of approach that the US, with its **penchant for black and white**, is most uncomfortable with.

International affairs are always a combination of the egos, pride, and desires of people and nations, and the sad fact is that even at this very moment, while killing is going on in Ukraine, many nations are watching the situation while calculating the advantages for their own country.

It was this situation that eventually led to the warfare that **engulfed** the entire world in the last two world wars. At the very least, we need to keep a close watch on the actions of our own government so that we can learn from these lessons and prevent Russia from **running amok**.

国の進出もあってか、コロナパンデミックによる経済的ダメージどころか、街にはこれまで以上の活気すら感じられ、マニラの気の遠くなるような**渋滞**を解消するインフラ工事も着実に進んでいます。

こうした将来性のある国々に、今回のロシアへの制裁措置は新たな**経済的打撃**を与えるかもしれません。とすれば、中国としてはあからさまな欧米主要国との対立構造を作らずに、静かにこうした地域への経済的な潤いを与え続ける戦術に終始した方が得策かもしれません。中国はその判断の是非を自問しているはずです。

ヘッドラインのように、バイデン大統領が中国の習近平主席に、電話会談でロシアを援助しないように警告したというニュースが伝わりました。しかし、大切なことは、こうした中国のデリケートな状況を考えながら、彼らを追い込まないようにそっと状況を見ておく方が、対ロシア戦略としては得策かもしれません。しかし、こうしたアプローチは、**白黒をはっきりさせたがる**アメリカが最も苦手なことなのです。

国際問題は常に人々や国々のエゴとプライド、そして欲望が重なって、ウクライナで殺戮が進んでいる今この瞬間でも、多くの国が自国のためのそろばんを弾きながら、情勢を見ているという悲しい実情があります。

こうした状況が、最終的に世界中を**巻き込む戦乱**へと発展したのが、先の二つの世界大戦に他なりません。少なくともその教訓に多くの人が目を向けながら、ロシアの**暴走**を防ぐことができるよう、自らの政府の動きを注視してゆく必要があるのです。

Key word

EXPANISION 拡大、展開

　何かの「量や範囲を増やす動き、拡大した部分」を表し、本文では中国によるアジアへの「進出」の訳語となっています。動詞はexpandです。同じような意味でadvanceやadvancement（前進、発展）という言葉も、economic advancement（経済進出）などの形で使われています。

　アジアだけにとどまらず、ヨーロッパやアフリカにまで経済的・軍事的進出を図っている中国、そして軍事大国であり人口の増加に伴う経済力の発展も目覚ましいインドの動きを、今後も注視し続けていく必要がありそうです。

例文

The China's goal is expansion into the South China Sea.
中国の狙いは南シナ海への進出だ。

In an attempt to expand market share, our company tried to buy out the competition.
市場シェアを拡大するために、当社は競合他社を買収しようとした。

The country's economic advancement has been remarkable in recent years.
近年、その国の経済は目覚ましい発展を遂げている。

❓ あなたはどう答える？

What has the Japanese government's response to Russia's invasion of Ukraine been?
ロシアによるウクライナ侵攻に、日本政府はどのような対応をしていますか？

ヒント ウクライナに対して人道的・財政的支援や避難民の受け入れを行うとともに、ロシアには政府関係者の資産凍結、ビザ発給の停止などの制裁措置をとっています。

覚えておくと便利な単語、表現

☐ announce support for　〜への支援を表明する

☐ impose economic sanctions on　〜に経済制裁を課す

☐ maintain cooperative ties with　〜との協力関係を維持する

第4話
ウクライナ問題の背景に見える プロテスタンティズムのビジネス観

Article 4
Protestantism's View of Business in the Context of the Ukraine Issue

Business is business. Nothing personal.

—— アメリカの格言

（ビジネスはビジネス、個人的なことではないさ）

Business is business. Nothing personal.

This is a phrase often used in the US.

This is the point that Japanese people are most likely to misunderstand when they think about **world affairs**.

When the topic of World War II came up, someone commented that he still wonders why Japan went to war with the US. I told him, "the US won the war against Japan because it approached it as business," but it was difficult for him to understand the true meaning of my comment.

In fact, the answer to this question reveals the background of the conflict between Russia and the US over Ukraine. The phrase "war is a business" is a great **perspective** from which to analyze international affairs.

Luther, who initiated the Protestant Reformation in 1517, protested that it was wrong for the Roman Catholic Church to intervene between God and the individual. He argued that God and the individual should be directly connected by faith, and that there should be no authority or power enjoying privileges between them. This protest was supported by princes, who at the time were reluctant to accept the authority of the **papacy**, and the storm of the Reformation spread throughout Europe. The new religion that emerged was Protestantism.

Protestantism transformed the Netherlands and England, and **persecuted** people from the old continent migrated to the new continent, giving birth to the nation of the US. In other words, the origins of American consciousness lie in Protestant beliefs and **principles of action**. As immigrants from around the world became accustomed to American society, they were strongly influenced by it, even though their ideological beliefs

► business → p.48

ビジネスはビジネス、個人的なことではない。

これはアメリカでよく使われる言葉です。

世界情勢を考える上で、日本人が最も誤解しやすい点がこの一言の中に隠されています。

第二次世界大戦の話題が出たとき、どうしてアメリカと戦争にまでなったのか今でも不思議だ、というコメントがありました。そこで私は「アメリカはビジネスとして日本に勝ったのですよ」と言ったのですが、相手にはその真意がなかなか伝わりませんでした。

実はこの問いへの答えを見ると、そこにウクライナをめぐるロシアとアメリカとの対立の背景までがあぶり出されます。「戦争はビジネス」というこの言葉が、国際情勢を分析する上での大きな**視点**となるのです。

1517年に宗教改革を始めたルターは、ローマ・カトリック教会が神と個人との間に介在し、そこに君臨するのはおかしいと抗議しました。神と個人とは直接信仰でつながるべきで、その間にどんな権威も権力も存在して**特権を享受する**べきではないと唱えたのです。その抗議が、当時**ローマ教皇**の権威を煙たがっていた諸侯に支持され、宗教改革の嵐がヨーロッパ中に広がりました。こうしてできあがった新教が、プロテスタントです。

マルティン・ルター

プロテスタントはオランダやイギリスを変革し、旧大陸で**迫害された**人々は新大陸へと移住し、アメリカという国家が誕生しました。つまりアメリカ人の意識の原点は、プロテスタントとしての信仰のあり方や**行動原理**にあります。世界中からの移民もアメリカ社会に馴染むに従って、思想信条や信仰こそ違うものの、その影響を強く受けてゆくのです。

Article 4

and faith were different.

The principle behind Protestant people's behavior is that as long as an individual has faith and is directly connected to God, their actions are **not subject to any restrictions**, and they can pursue their own happiness **at their own risk**. In other words, the idea that working and earning wealth are not bad things and that pursuing business is a natural right of the individual became established.

This awareness was the starting point for the development of the UK and the US as **economic powers**. In the process, they began to separate personal feelings from business interactions in order to conduct business more effectively. As the term "businesslike" suggests, business is business, whether you like the person you are working with personally or not.

This concept **permeates** the implementation of national policies and military actions as well. In other words, **diplomatic maneuvering** and economic activities are business, not driven by personal likes, dislikes, or feelings.

Thus, when Japan and the US were **at odds** over interests in China and other countries before World War II, the US tried to win the negotiations as a business. Japan, however, had absorbed economic, political, and military know-how from the West as an institution, but it did not have a business-like mindset that originated from a Protestant consciousness. Japanese emotions drove them into a war that was impossible to win. As a result, Japan was integrated into the US economic sphere through the **defeat in the war**. The US invested in Japan through the war and reaped the benefits of that investment.

　プロテスタントの人々の行動原理は、個人が信仰を持ち、直接神とつながっている以上、個人の行動は**どんな制約も受けず、自己の責任で**自分の幸福を追求することができるというものです。言い換えれば、仕事をして富を得ることは悪いことではなく、ビジネスを追求することは個人の当然の権利だという考え方が定着します。

　この意識がイギリスやアメリカが**経済大国**として発展する原点でした。そして、その過程で彼らはビジネス的な行為をより効果的に実践するために、個人的な感情とビジネスでのやり取りとを分離するようになりました。「ビジネスライク」という言葉があるように、仕事相手が個人的に好きであろうとなかろうと、ビジネスはビジネスとして実践されるのです。

　この考え方は、国の政策の実行や軍事行為などにも**浸透**します。つまり、**外交的な駆け引き**や経済的活動はビジネスで、個人の好悪や感情に左右されるものではないのです。

　ですから、戦前に中国などでの利権を巡って日本とアメリカが**対立した**ときも、アメリカはビジネスとしてその駆け引きに勝利しようとしました。しかし、日本は制度として経済や政治軍事活動のノウハウは欧米から吸収したものの、プロテスタントの意識を原点とするビジネスライクなものの考え方は持てませんでした。日本人としての感情が、勝利することが不可能な戦争へと駆り立てたのです。その結果、**敗戦**を通して、日本はアメリカの経済圏に組み込まれます。アメリカは戦争を通して日本に投資し、それを回収して余りある恩恵を享受したわけです。

This also applies to the Ukraine issue. From the US perspective, the Ukrainian issue is a **triumph** of business strategy by the West that has led Ukraine to announce its intention to join NATO and the EU.

In contrast, Protestantism has not been nurtured in Russia. When Russia was transformed from an imperialist regime supported by **serfdom** into a communist state, there was no climate there to nurture business as business. The state continued to be run by an **authoritarian** system and those who followed it, and the majority of the population accepted this structure. After the collapse of the Soviet Union, Russia embraced **capitalism**, but so-called business-like, free economic activity never prevailed.

Therefore, instead of having a business-oriented strategy to control Ukraine within its own economic sphere, Russia could only appeal to nationalistic sentiments in response to the erosion of its own influence in Ukraine, which led to the current invasion. It was a **fatal choice** for Russia.

Now, Protestants and those who are influenced by Protestantism are trying to connect globally through business strategies.

However, there are many problems in the process. Business is an act of making money, so if the supply of gas from Russia is reduced, they will change their policies quite easily in order to find **alternatives**. Whether it is the supply of oil from Iran or the reduction of oil production in the Middle East, their policy decisions are based on how profitable it is for them. The political influence of the energy business, which generates enormous profits, and of the financial business that invests in it, is **immeasurable**. Japan should better understand the complexity of these

　これはウクライナ問題にも当てはまります。ウクライナ問題をアメリカから見た場合、ウクライナがNATOやEUに加盟することを表明するまでになったのは、西側諸国によるビジネス上の戦略の**勝利**です。

　対して、ロシアではプロテスタンティズムは育っていません。ロシアは**農奴制**に支えられた帝政から共産主義国家になったとき、そこにビジネスをビジネスとして育てる風土は皆無でした。その後も、**権威**とそれに従う人々とが織りなす構造によって国家が運営され、大多数の国民もそれを受け入れてきました。ソ連崩壊のあと、ロシアは**資本主義**を受け入れますが、いわゆるビジネスライクで自由な経済活動が流布することはありませんでした。

　従って、ロシアはウクライナを自らの経済圏の中でコントロールするための、ビジネスとして割り切った戦略を持つ代わりに、自らの影響力がウクライナから削がれてゆくことに対して、ナショナリズム的な感情に訴えることしかできず、今回の侵攻を行いました。それはロシアにとって**致命的な選択**でした。

西欧化を強力に推進する一方で農奴制を強化したピョートル1世。プーチン大統領が尊敬する人物

　今、プロテスタント的な意識を基盤に持った人々と、その影響を受けた人々は、ビジネス戦略によってグローバルにつながろうとしています。

　ただ、その過程で様々な問題も発生しています。ビジネスとはお金を儲ける行為ですから、ロシアからガスの供給が減少すれば、その**代替**を探すために、彼らはいとも簡単に政策を転換します。イランからの原油の供給も、中東の石油の減産も、彼らにとってはそれがどのような利益につながるかが政策判断の基準になります。莫大な利益を生み出すエネルギービジネスと、そ

international affairs more fundamentally.

    The world has become more democratic and livable due to these business-like practices, and at the same time, it has become more **divided** and distrustful due to the inhibitions and selfishness that come from separating business and individuals too much. These contradictions constantly **play havoc with** the world, and in many cases have led to chaos that is sometimes unrecognizable.

    When analyzing critical phenomena occurring in the world, isn't it necessary to have a calm perspective that looks at things from such a historical background?

こに投資している金融ビジネスが政治に与える影響は**計り知れません**。日本もこうした国際情勢の複雑さをもっとその本質的なところから理解するべきです。

　世界にはこうしたビジネスライクな行為によって、より民主的で住みやすくなった部分と、逆に余りにもビジネスと個人とを切り離しすぎることから生まれる阻害や利己的な行為によって、人々が**分断され**、不信感を抱き合うという負の部分とが同居しています。その矛盾が常に世界を**翻弄し**、ときには収集のつかない混乱へとつながった事例も多くあります。

　世界で起きている危機的な現象を分析するときに、こうした歴史的な背景から物事を見てゆく冷静な視点も必要ではないでしょうか。

Key word

BUSINESS　ビジネス、事業

　日本語では「ビジネス」と一口に表しますが、実にさまざまな意味を持つ言葉です。商業や経済活動全般を指す場合もあれば、一件あたりの商取引や売買を指すこともあり、自分が従事する特定の業種や業界、職業も表します。ちなみに、日本語で「ビジネスマン」というと商業に従事する人全般を指しますが、英語の businessman（businessperson）は「実業家、経営者」を指し、その人たちが利用する少し高級なホテルや飛行機を business hotel、business class といいます。Business には「私事」の意味もあり、That's my business.(それは私の問題です)/ That's none of your business.（あなたには関係ない）といった形で使われます。

....

例文

The interests of our company and the client were aligned and the business was launched.
当社と取引先との利害が一致して、その事業が立ち上がった。

My business is going well.
私の仕事は順調だ。

The latest tax hike hit small businesses much harder than it did major companies.
今回の増税は、大企業よりも中小企業に大きな打撃を与えた。

 あなたはどう答える？

What do the Japanese value in business?
日本人がビジネスで大事にしていることは何ですか？

> ヒント　日本型ビジネス文化の特徴として、時間を厳守する、組織のコンセンサスを重視する、上下関係を重んじる、品質を大切にする、ことなどがよく挙げられます。

覚えておくと便利な単語、表現

☐ **consensus decision making**　合意による意思決定
☐ **punctual culture**　時間を守る文化
☐ **respect the hierarchical relationship**　上下関係を重んじる

第5話
ディアスポラと国際政治

Article 5
Diaspora and International Politics

By the end of the 1980s the number of Chinese-speaking students in the United States was about 90,000, easily the largest number of any ethnic group. At that point the Taiwanese alone accounted for roughly one in every four candidates for doctorates in electrical engineering in the United States.

—— Joel Kotkin, *Tribes*

（1980年代末には、アメリカにいる中国語圏の学生数は約9万人となり、あらゆる民族の中で最も多くなった。この時点で、台湾人だけでアメリカの電気工学の博士号候補者の4人に1人を占めるに至っていた）

When asked why China has not invaded Taiwan while Russia is attacking Ukraine, many people point to the high risk involved.

First, there is the view that China is **reluctant to** do so because of the strong **solidarity** it saw among the Western nations during the invasion of Ukraine. There is also the view that China's suppression of speech in Hong Kong, Uyghur, and other areas has led to tensions with the US and other countries, and that it is a risk to add more fuel to the fire.

Furthermore, the Chinese economy has **stalled** due to China's adherence to the zero-COVID policy, which, along with its isolation in foreign affairs, has been a **major blow** to the Xi Jinping administration, which may be hoping to maintain power without causing any problems.

However, there is another major perspective missing here.

That is the existence of a "diaspora," a large **network** of humanity that transcends national boundaries. Diaspora is a word that means the **dispersion** of peoples. Originally, it referred to people of Jewish descent spreading around the world while maintaining their own identity and has also come to refer to people who have emigrated from their homeland for a variety of reasons.

The intersection of 5th Avenue and 47th Street in New York City is known as the "Diamond District," and is a famous place where diamonds from all over the world are traded. The people engaged in the diamond trade here are typical of the Jewish diaspora. They have connections that transcend borders, and they use them for trading and sometimes for forming political

▶ network ➜ p.58

ロシアがウクライナに攻撃をしかけているとき、なぜ中国は台湾に侵攻しないのかという問いに、多くの人はそのリスクの大きさを指摘します。

まず、ウクライナ侵攻のときに西側諸国が見せた強い**結束**を目にした中国が**及び腰**になっているという見方があります。また、中国は香港やウイグルなどでの言論弾圧によってアメリカなどと緊張関係にあり、これ以上火に油を注ぐことはリスクだという判断ではないかという見方もあります。

しかも、ゼロコロナ政策への固執から中国経済は**失速**し、外交での孤立と共に習近平政権にとっては**痛手が大きい**ことから、このまま問題を起こさずなんとか政権を維持してゆきたいという意向もあるのでしょう。

しかし、ここに欠けているもう一つの大きな視点があります。

それは「ディアスポラ」という国家を超えた人類の大きなネットワークの存在です。ディアスポラというのは、民族の**離散**を意味する言葉です。元々は、ユダヤ系の人々が自らのアイデンティティをもって世界に拡散していることを指し、様々な理由で祖国から移住してきた人々のことも指すようになりました。

ニューヨークの5番街と47丁目が交差したあたりは「ダイヤモンド街」といわれ、世界中のダイヤが取引される有名な場所です。ここでダイヤモンドの取引に従事する人々は典型的なユダヤ系のディアスポラです。彼らは国境を越えてつながり、取引をし、時には政治的にもネットワークします。

networks.

In China, too, from the middle of the 19th century onwards, during a **period of turmoil** caused by the invasion of the great powers and domestic revolutionary movements, many Chinese people spread out into the world, creating a diaspora. With financial support from this network, Sun Yat-sen risked his life to lead the Xinhai Revolution to overthrow the Qing dynasty in 1911-1912.

After the war, when a **communist regime** came to power in China, many Chinese who had **aspired to** become democracies formed a new diaspora. One aspect of Taiwan is that it is protected by the funds transferred by these people. Overseas Chinese who support Taiwan are spread throughout Asia, including Japan, the US, and Europe, and are connected across national borders. Moreover, even in the countries where they **reside**, the successful ones lobby governments, and sometimes even work within the governments themselves.

Similar networks exist for those who have spread around the world from India, Russia, the Middle East, and elsewhere, and these invisible networks of diaspora influence international politics in complex ways.

For example, it is well known that Ukrainian President Zelensky is of Jewish descent. Moreover, Russia is known for its persistent **discrimination** against Jews from the imperial period to the present. If so, it is easy to understand why Israel and its **ally**, the US, opposed Russia when it invaded Ukraine. Like the network in New York's Diamond District, it can mobilize the world's economies to oppose Russia.

The backgrounds of people in the diaspora are not uniform.

　中国でも19世紀の中盤以降、列強の侵略と国内の革命運動という**混乱期**に、多くの中国人が世界に拡散し、ディアスポラとなりました。このネットワークから経済的なサポートを受け、1911年から1912年にかけて清朝を倒そうと命懸けで辛亥革命を指導したのが孫文でした。

孫文

　戦後になって中国に**共産主義政権**が誕生すると、民主主義国家を**目指していた**中国人の多くが新たなディアスポラを形成します。そんな彼らの動かす資金によって、台湾が守られているという一面があるのです。台湾を支持する華僑はアメリカやヨーロッパ、日本を含むアジア各地に拡散し、国境を越えてつながります。さらに、それぞれが**居住する**国でも成功した者は政府へのロビー活動を行い、時には政府の中でも活動します。

　同様のネットワークはインド、ロシア、中東などから世界に拡散した人々にもあり、こうしたディアスポラの見えないネットワークが複雑に国際政治に影響を与えているのです。
　例えば、ウクライナのゼレンスキー大統領がユダヤ系であることは有名な話です。しかも、ロシアは帝政時代から現在にかけて、執拗にユダヤ人**差別**をしてきたことで知られています。であれば、ロシアがウクライナに侵攻したとき、イスラエルとその**同盟国**アメリカがロシア包囲網を作ったことは容易に頷けます。ニューヨークのダイヤモンド街でのネットワークのように、世界中の経済を動かしてロシアに対抗することができるのです。
　ディアスポラの人々の背景は一様ではありません。ア

Both in the US and in Europe, these people's backgrounds are **skillfully** used to gather information, and sometimes even to communicate with their home countries.

Therefore, China cannot easily invade Taiwan. It knows better than anyone how the **dynasties** that controlled and suppressed speech were destroyed by the Xinhai Revolution, a movement supported by a diaspora network. All of them worry that the ends of this network may reach under their own government.

When people became fearful of these transnational networks, they sometimes talked about **conspiracy theories** and began to oppress such peoples.

The conspiracy theory that Jewish people rule the world from behind the scenes is particularly well known, and it became a concrete policy in its extreme form with Hitler's **genocidal** acts against the Jews (the Holocaust).

Something similar happened in America. In the 20th century, anti-Chinese and anti-Japanese immigration laws were **enacted** against immigrants from those countries, and there were times when they were unfairly discriminated against. Behind this was the "Yellow Peril" theory, which claimed that Asian races were

メリカでもヨーロッパでも、こうした人々の背景を**巧み**
に利用しながら情報を収集し、さらに時には彼らの本国
とのやりとりも行うのです。

　ですから、中国は台湾に簡単には侵攻できません。言
論を統制弾圧していた中国の王朝が、ディアスポラのネ
ットワークによって支援された運動から辛亥革命に至っ
て滅亡した経緯を、彼らは誰よりも知っているからです。
このネットワークの末端が自らの政府の足元にも及んで
いるかもしれないことは、彼らの誰もが気にしているこ
となのです。

　こうした国境を越えたネットワークに恐怖心を抱くと
き、人々は**陰謀論**を語り、そうした民族への弾圧を始め
ることもありました。

　ユダヤ系の人々が世界を陰で支配しているという陰謀
論は特に有名で、それが極端な形で具体的な政策となっ
たのが、ヒトラーによるユダヤ人への**虐殺行為**（ホロコー
スト）でした。

　似たようなことはアメリカでも起こりました。20世紀
になって、中国や日本からの移民に対する排中移民法、排
日移民法などが**制定され**、不当な差別をしたことがあり
ました。その背景にあったのが、アジアの黄色人種がヨ
ーロッパ文明を**侵食している**という「黄禍論」で、それ

「黄禍」という言葉を世界に知らしめた寓意画
『ヨーロッパの諸国民よ、諸君らの最も神聖な
宝を守れ』は、ドイツ帝国のヴィルヘルム2世に
よって広められた。日清戦争による日本の中国
大陸進出を契機にロシア・ドイツ・フランスを
はじめとする欧州に広がった。

encroaching on European civilization. It spread to Germany and other European countries and had a considerable impact on the US as well.

These conspiracy theories can mislead people in seemingly persuasive ways and are sometimes even used to heighten nationalism.

When looking at these global trends, the Japanese have one characteristic in common. It is the thinness of the network with which the Japanese diaspora has spread around the world.

Both before and after World War II, the Japanese tended to forget those who went out from the country and did not value information from them. Some have even pointed out that this is one of the reasons for Japan's **poor diplomacy**. Japan's policy of creating groups only within Japan, distinguishing between Japan as "inside" and the rest of the world as "outside," has led to misreading of world affairs many times in the past.

It is extremely important to **decipher** the intersection of diaspora networks and the national interests of each nation in order to understand the global situation in the future.

はドイツをはじめとしたヨーロッパに拡散し、アメリカにも少からぬ影響を与えました。

　こうした陰謀論は、一見すると説得力をもって人々を惑わし、時にはナショナリズムの高揚にまで利用されることがあるのです。

　こうした世界の動きを見るときに、日本人は一つの特徴を持っています。それは世界に拡散した日本人のディアスポラとのネットワークの希薄さです。

　戦前も戦後も、日本人は外に出ていった人々を忘れがちで、そこからの情報を大切にはしませんでした。これが日本人の**外交下手**の一つの原因であるという指摘もあるほどです。日本を「内」、そして海外を「外」として区別し、「内」だけでグループを作る日本の政策が、過去に何度も世界情勢を読み誤る原因を作りました。

　ディアスポラのネットワークとそれぞれの国家の国益との交錯を**読み解く**ことが、これからの世界情勢を見つめてゆく上でも、極めて重要なことなのです。

NETWORK 網、人脈

　もともと「網状につくられたもの」全般を指し、そこから派生して人脈やラジオ・テレビの放送網、通信のネットワークも表します。動詞では「他の人と関わりを持つ、人脈を保つ」という意味です。

　本文では「ディアスポラ（diaspora）」という離散・移住した人々が国境を越えてつながり、そのネットワークが世界の政治や経済に影響を及ぼすことが述べられています。世界情勢を読むにあたって、こうしたネットワークと国益とのつながりを鑑みることが、日本の外交に求められているのです。

例文

He is building up a network of acquaintances outside his office.
彼は社外で人脈を築いている。

Our job is to connect the computers to the network.
私たちの仕事はコンピュータをネットワークに接続することだ。

You have to network if you want to get a good position.
よいポジションに就きたいのであれば、人脈を広げなければならない。

？ あなたはどう答える？

Please tell us about the diaspora of Japanese people that migrated abroad.
日本から海外に移住したディアスポラについて教えてください。

ヒント　日本人の労働移民は主に明治以降、ハワイや北米・中南米、さらに朝鮮や台湾、満州へと渡りました。彼らやその子孫の日系人は現在も約400万人いると推定されています。

覚えておくと便利な単語、表現

☐ migrant worker　外国への出稼ぎ労働者

☐ migrate　〔人が経済的理由で他の国や地域へ〕移住する

☐ people of Japanese descent　日系の人々

第2章

アメリカ外交と
民主主義

Chapter 2

US Diplomacy and
Democracy

第6話
波紋を呼んだ国際社会での
アメリカ大統領の発言

Article 6
Remarks by the President of the United States to the International Community Cause Controversy

Biden says Vladimir Putin "Cannot remain in power"
White House quickly tries to walk back comment
—— CNN

（バイデンが「ウラディーミル・プーチンは権力の座に残るべきではない」と発言。ホワイトハウスは即座にその発言を抑制するコメントを発表）

President Biden delivered a speech **condemning** Russia's invasion of Ukraine during a visit to Poland. In that speech, he said that Putin "cannot remain in power," which caused an unexpected stir.

Immediately afterward, the White House **issued a statement** on the remarks, making the unusual correction that "the Russian people themselves should decide whether President Putin should step down." The American media also invited **intellectuals** to discuss the president's remarks in order to question his true intentions.

From these reactions in the US, we can see another aspect behind Russia's invasion of Ukraine.

The situation reminds us of the **confrontation** between the US and the Soviet Union during the Cold War. There is only one reason that those days were called the "Cold War": the US and the Soviet Union, both nuclear **superpowers**, did not engage in direct combat.

Even during the Cold War era, actual wars, or "hot wars," took place all over the world. Both the US and the Soviet Union were directly involved in the wars, trying to maintain their influence. The Vietnam War that began in 1954 and the Soviet invasion of Afghanistan in 1978 were examples of these.

In fact, the US has been involved in the **overthrow** of foreign **regimes** by force many times in the past: when an elected socialist government came to power in Chile in 1973, the US manipulated the Chilean military to **topple** the then-Allende government in a coup d'état. When a pro-Soviet regime came to power in the small Caribbean Island nation of Grenada, the US sent troops to

▶ regime ➙ p.68

　バイデン大統領が、ポーランド訪問中にロシアのウク
ライナ侵攻を**非難する**演説を行いました。その演説の中
で「プーチン大統領は権力の座からおりるべきだ」と言
ったことが、思わぬ波紋を呼びました。

　ホワイトハウスは、その直後にこの発言について**声明
を発表し**、「プーチン大統領の去就は、ロシア国民自身が
決めるべきだ」という異例の訂正を行ったのです。そし
てアメリカの各メディアも、大統領の発言について真意
を問いただそうと、**識者**が招かれ議論をしていました。

ジョー・バイデン米大統領

　こうしたアメリカ国内の反応から、ロシアのウクライナ
侵攻の背景にあるもう一つの側面を見ていきましょう。

　ロシアのウクライナ侵攻は冷戦時代のアメリカとソ連
との**対立**を思い出させます。当時のことをなぜ「冷戦(冷
たい戦争)」と言ったかというと、たった一つの理由、つ
まり、核を保有する**超大国**であったアメリカとソ連とが、
直接戦火を交えなかったことに尽きるのです。

　冷戦時代にも実際の戦争、つまり戦火を交えた「熱い
戦争」は世界各地で起こっていました。その戦争にアメ
リカもソ連も直接関与しながら、双方の影響力を維持し
ようとしていました。その代表が1954年に始まったベト
ナム戦争であり、1978年に起きたソ連によるアフガニス
タン侵攻だったのです。

　実はアメリカも過去に何度も力によって海外の**政権**の
転覆に関わっていました。1973年に南米のチリで選挙に
よる社会主義政権が誕生したとき、アメリカはチリの軍
部を操り、チリ軍のクーデターによって当時のアジェン
デ政権を**崩壊**させました。カリブ海の小さな島国グレナ
ダに親ソ政権が生まれると、1983年にアメリカが**宣戦布**

overthrow that regime without a **declaration of war** in 1983. In late 1989 and 1990, the US invaded Panama and used force to capture General Noriega, the de facto ruler of the country at the time, and tried him in US courts for openly **smuggling** drugs to the US.

Furthermore, after the end of the Cold War, the US invaded Iraq in 2003 on the grounds that Iraq possessed biological and chemical weapons and was planning terrorist activities, over-throwing the regime of Saddam Hussein.

The background of these wars and incidents is complex, and it may not be possible to **unilaterally** condemn the US for in-vading another country and engaging in political regime change there by force. It may also be argued that Russia's invasion of Ukraine is different in nature from these past events.

However, it seems to be true that the US, now self-identified as the **standard-bearer** of freedom and democracy, is extreme-ly sensitive about reminding the rest of the world of former American actions and mistakes.

When Russia invaded Ukraine, there was outrage from around the world.

However, it is also true that there are many people in Africa, Asia, and Latin America who have distanced themselves a bit from such voices. This is because they have memories of America's past actions and a cynical view of America's loud ad-vocacy of freedom and democracy. Russia is well aware that there are countries that see things that way. So is China.

President Biden's statement was a brazen move that showed the arrogance of the US. Regardless of what Russia's arrogance may have been, it was not good for either the US government

告なしに軍隊を送り、その政権を転覆させました。また、1989年末から90年にかけて、アメリカに対して麻薬の**密輸出**を公然と行っていたとして、アメリカはパナマに侵攻し、武力で当時の事実上の支配者であるノリエガ将軍を拘束し、アメリカの法廷で裁きました。

アメリカ軍に拘束されたマヌエル・ノリエガ

さらに、冷戦終結後には、イラクが生物化学兵器を保持しテロ活動を目論んでいるとして、2003年にアメリカはイラクに侵攻し、当時のサダム・フセイン政権を転覆させたことは記憶に新しいはずです。

これらの戦争や事件の背景は複雑で、アメリカが他国に侵攻し、力によってそこの政治体制の変更に関わったことを、**一方的に**非難することはできないかもしれません。また、ロシアによるウクライナ侵攻は、これらの過去の事案とは性質が異なるものだという議論もあるでしょう。

アメリカのイラク侵攻後に倒されるサダム・フセインの像

ただ、今アメリカが自由と民主主義の**旗手**であると自認している中で、かつてのアメリカの行為や過ちを世界の国々が思い出すことについて、極めて敏感になっていることは事実のようです。

ロシアがウクライナに侵攻したとき、世界中から怒りの声が上がりました。

しかし、アフリカやアジア、そして中南米の国々の中には、そうした声に少し距離を置いている人々が多くいることも事実です。その背景には、彼らの中にアメリカの過去の行いへの記憶があり、アメリカが自由や民主主義を声高に唱えることへのシニカルな視線があるからに他なりません。ロシアはそうした視線が世界にあることを熟知しています。それは中国も同様です。

バイデン大統領の発言は、こうしたアメリカの傲慢な一面をついつい見せてしまった勇み足でした。ロシアがどのような横暴な行為に出ていようと、アメリカの大統

or the media to be reminded of the US's series of **aggressive interventions** in the international community during and after the Cold War by a US president explicitly telling the leader of another country to resign.

What we need to know is that the **subtle** response of the US government after this statement shows the problem of delicacy in international politics and diplomacy. In Japan, this issue is often overlooked and not covered much in the news. However, it is fundamental to the power of diplomacy to be able to **discern** how a leader or influential person intends to make a statement, how it will be perceived by other countries or people in other countries, and how an **adversary**, such as Russia or China, will use the statement to sway international opinion. Anticipating the complex effects of statements and actions and successfully putting out fires in advance are always necessary for resolving international issues.

From this point of view, when one looks at President Biden's remarks and the White House's subsequent response, the **exquisite** coordination at play, which would be unthinkable in Japanese politics, is impressive.

In other words, while President Biden used strong words to check Russia, the White House and the State Department once again reminded the world that they would never violate international law the way that Russia violated the sovereignty of other countries.

Why was the US nervous about the rashness of the US President in Poland? There is no other reason than that it was protecting its own **raison d'être** and the legitimacy of its past actions.

領が他国の指導者に対して「辞任しろ」と明言することによって、まさに冷戦時代とその後のアメリカによる一連の国際社会への**強引な介入**を思い起こさせることは、アメリカ政府にとってもマスコミにとっても好ましくないことだと映ったわけです。

　我々が知っておきたいことは、この発言の後の**微妙な**アメリカ政府の対応が示す、国際政治と外交でのデリカシーの問題です。日本ではともすれば見落とされ、ニュースでもそれほど取り上げられません。しかし、一人の指導者や影響力のある人物がどういった意図でその発言を行い、それを他の国や関係国の人々がどのように捉え、さらにロシアや中国といった**相手国**がその発言をどのように利用して国際世論に揺さぶりをかけてくるかといったことを、しっかりと**見極める**ことが外交力の基本です。発言や行為が生み出す複雑な影響を予測し、事前にうまく火消しをすることが国際問題を解決する上では常に必要とされています。

　その点から、今回のバイデン大統領の発言とホワイトハウスのその後の対応を見たときに、日本の政治では考えられないような**絶妙な**連携プレーがあったことに感心させられます。

　つまり、バイデン大統領が強い言葉でロシアを牽制しながら、ホワイトハウスや国務省は、ロシアが他国の主権を侵害したように、自らはそうした国際法違反は絶対にしないと、世界に向けて改めて釘を刺したのです。

　ポーランドで起きたアメリカ大統領の勇み足に、なぜアメリカがハラハラしたのか。それは自らの過去の行いも含め、アメリカそのものの**存在意義**とその正当性をあえて守りたかったからに他ならないからなのです。

第2章

Key word

REGIME　政治体制、政権

　もとはフランス語の"régime(レジーム)"からきており「統治・政府の形態や構造そのもの」を表しますが、ときに「(強権的な)政府・政権」というニュアンスが伴います。本文では冷戦時代から21世紀に至るまで幾度もくり返された、アメリカによる他国への軍事介入と政権転覆について述べています。ちなみに「転覆させる」はoverthrowといいます。アメリカは「民主主義(democracy)」そして「正義(justice)」を大義名分として、相対する社会主義政権や反米政権を倒してきた過去の歴史があります。そうした数々の行いから見える傲慢さゆえに、現在のアメリカに対して世界各国からシニカルな視線がブーメランのように注がれているのです。

例文

The Ancien Régime was the regime during the period of absolute monarchy before the French Revolution.
アンシャン・レジームとは、フランス革命前の絶対王政期の体制のことである。

The United States has repeatedly overthrown socialist regimes.
アメリカは社会主義政権を何度も転覆させてきた。

Myanmar's government was overthrown by a coup d'etat by the national army.
ミャンマー政府は国軍のクーデターによって転覆させられた。

 あなたはどう答える？

What would be the response if a Japanese politician made a controversial statement?
日本の政治家が物議を醸すような発言をしたらどのような対応がされますか？

ヒント　こうした発言はメディアで取り上げられ、ネット上で議論を呼びます。当事者が謝罪や撤回を述べますが、役職の辞任に追い込まれたり任命責任が問われることが多いです。

覚えておくと便利な単語、表現

□ **apologize and take one's remark back**　謝罪をして前言を撤回する
□ **controversy over someone's gaffes**　(人)の失言を巡る論争
□ **responsibility for appointing**　任命責任

第7話
「是は是、非は非」が通らない
複雑な2022年

Article 7
A Complicated 2022 in Which "Right Is Right, Wrong Is Wrong" Does Not Work

US and South Korea fire missiles after North Korea launches

―― CNN

（アメリカと韓国は北朝鮮が弾道弾を発射した直後にミサイルの発射で対応）

Article 7

Since Russia invaded Ukraine, the US has been **at the mercy of** an unprecedentedly complex set of challenges. The joint launch test of missiles by the US and South Korea, influenced by their concern over North Korea, may be an event that symbolizes the Biden administration's irritation over the situation.

In fact, the fundamentals of the US **foreign policy strategy**, which, as the standard-bearer of democracy, has been taking a "right is right, wrong is wrong" stance in an attempt to expand the rights that citizens should have, such as "freedom of speech," to the rest of the world, have been shaken.

In order to stop Russia's invasion of Ukraine, the world must respond **in unison**. To do so, the US has been forced to make major **compromises** with countries that it has criticized in the past as threatening democracy.

One example is the murder of Khashoggi, a journalist who had been at odds with the current Saudi regime, at the Saudi embassy in Turkey. The US took a strong stance against the **unprecedented brutality** of the murder of a journalist by a state power, and it developed into a situation where the foundations of the friendly relations between the two countries were shaken.

Russia, aware of this situation, deftly approached Saudi Arabia to sway Western Europe, which was trying to strengthen sanctions against Russia over its oil strategy. This situation forced the US to launch a **diplomatic effort** to improve relations with Saudi Arabia.

A similar situation occurred when Finland and Sweden applied to join NATO.

► compromise → p.76

　ロシアがウクライナに侵攻して以来、アメリカは過去にない複雑な課題に**翻弄**されています。アメリカと韓国による北朝鮮を意識したミサイルの合同発射実験は、そんな状況に対するバイデン政権の苛立ちを象徴したできごとなのかもしれません。

　実は、民主主義の旗手として、例えば「言論の自由」など国民が持つべき権利を世界に拡大させようとして、「是は是、非は非」というスタンスを取り続けてきたアメリカの**外交戦略**の根本が揺らいできているのです。

　ロシアのウクライナへの侵攻を止めるためには、世界中が**一致団結して**対応しなければなりません。そのためには、アメリカが過去に民主主義を脅かしていると批判してきた国々とも大きな**妥協**を強いられているわけです。

　一例が、サウジアラビアの現政権と対立していたジャーナリストのカショギ氏が、トルコにあるサウジアラビア大使館で殺害された事件です。ジャーナリストを国家権力が殺害するという**前代未聞の暴挙**に、アメリカは強い姿勢で臨み、それまでの両国の友好関係の礎が揺らぐ事態へと発展しました。

　この状況を知っているロシアは、したたかにサウジアラビアに歩み寄り、石油戦略でロシアへの制裁を強化しようとしている西欧に揺さぶりをかけたのです。そうした事態を受け、アメリカも慌ててサウジアラビアとの関係改善に向けた**外交努力**を始動させざるを得なくなりました。

　似たような状況は、フィンランドとスウェーデンがNATOへの加盟を申請したときにも起こりました。

第2章

Turkey, a member of NATO, was reluctant to allow both countries to join. This was in response to growing criticism by the Scandinavian countries of Turkey's oppression of the Kurds in Turkey. In order to **mediate** this situation, the Biden administration dared to intervene.

Russia once again has its eyes firmly fixed on the contradiction of the US, which has continuously criticized China for unfairly oppressing the Uyghurs, being forced to compromise on the Turkish situation. Turkey now prides itself on being the only diplomatic window to Russia and is trying to use it as a powerful card in its own diplomatic strategy.

And, as if to **mock** America's difficult position, North Korea has been conducting frequent **ballistic missile** tests. As if in response, the US and South Korea jointly conducted **interceptor missile** tests. Not wanting tensions to flare up in the Far East, the US is anxious to deal with this issue.

These problems that the US must deal with are coming in like a tsunami, sweeping across the world at once. The US, which has consistently placed the protection of democratic values as the basis of its foreign policy, saying that "right is right and wrong is wrong," now has to cooperate with the rest of the world for its policy toward Russia, while **turning a blind eye to** some issues.

Of course, responding to the food crisis and **soaring** prices caused by the Ukraine crisis is also an **urgent matter**. As soaring prices threaten the lives of Americans, dissatisfaction is mounting among the public. The Biden Administration needs some sort of secret recipe to deal with these complex puzzles in order to maintain political power. However, if it cannot find the

NATOのメンバーであるトルコが、国内でクルド人を弾圧しているとして北欧諸国が批判を強めていた状況を踏まえ、両国のNATOへの加盟に難色を示したのです。この状況を**調停する**ために、バイデン政権はあえてトルコに歩み寄らなければならなくなりました。

中国がウイグル人を不当に抑圧していると批判を続けてきたアメリカが、トルコの状況に対しては妥協を強いられているという矛盾を、ロシアはまたもしたたかに見つめています。トルコは、今ではロシアとの唯一の外交上の窓口であることを自負し、自らの外交戦略の強力なカードにしようとしています。

そして、そうしたアメリカの苦しい立場を**あざ笑う**かのように、北朝鮮も頻繁に**弾道ミサイル**の発射実験をくり返しています。それに対抗するかのように、アメリカと韓国が共同して**迎撃ミサイル**の発射実験を行ったわけです。極東に緊張が飛び火してほしくないアメリカとしては、この課題の対応に焦っています。

このようにアメリカが対応しなければならない問題が、津波のように世界各地で一気に押し寄せてきています。「是は是、非は非」として、一貫して民主主義の価値観を守ることを外交政策の基本に置いてきたアメリカが、一部の課題**には目をつぶり**ながら、対ロシア政策のために世界と連携してゆかなければならなくなったのです。

当然、ウクライナ危機に起因した食糧危機や物価の高騰への対応も、**喫緊**の課題です。物価の高騰でアメリカ人の生活が脅かされるなか、国民の間には不満が募っています。バイデン政権にとって、これらの複雑なパズルを解きながら政権運営を遂行するには、相当の秘策が必要です。しかし、そうした**特効薬**が見出せないままに、世

▶クルド人はトルコ・イラク北部・イラン北西部・シリア北東部などにまたがるクルディスタンに居住する民族。独自の言語と文化を持つが「国を持たない最大の民族」で、各国では少数派として差別や弾圧を受けている。

第2章

magic bullet it requires, it will likely be busy trying to cope with the world's turmoil.

Moreover, the soaring prices caused by Russia's invasion of Ukraine are becoming a critical situation that is directly fueling **social unrest**. Even if Russia does not dare to take strong action against the world, if the war becomes prolonged and if it can endure sanctions from the international community, Western policies toward Russia will naturally collapse. The same is true of China, which has been **eerily** reticent to perform on the diplomatic stage.

Even if public opinion in the US is unanimous in terms of sympathy for Ukraine, as a practical matter it is unacceptable for the economy to be further disrupted. Moreover, if the US is to **take a hard line against Russia** with the world on its side, it will have no choice but to change its existing foreign policy and seek compromises with many countries. Furthermore, in order to avoid further global turmoil, the problems of China and North Korea must be **weighed against** the situation in Ukraine.

The Biden administration faces a more complex set of contradictory and confusing foreign and domestic challenges than any previous administration.

界の混乱への対処療法に追われているのが、アメリカの現状なのかもしれません。

　しかも、ロシアのウクライナ侵攻による物価の高騰は、**社会不安を直接煽る危機的な状況**になりつつあります。ロシアとしては、あえて世界に対して強い行動に出なくても、戦争が長期化し、国際社会からの制裁に耐えられさえすれば、欧米の対ロシア政策は自ずと壊れてゆくのではと考えます。それは中国も同様で、中国もロシアも**不気味なほど**に外交の舞台でのパフォーマンスを控えています。

　ウクライナへの同情という意味ではアメリカの世論は一致していても、現実の問題として、これ以上経済が混乱することは受け入れられません。しかも、世界を味方につけて**対露強硬路線を貫こう**とするなら、それは今までの外交方針を転換して、多くの国々との妥協を模索せざるを得なくなります。さらに、これ以上世界が混乱しないようにするためには、中国と北朝鮮の問題をウクライナ情勢と**天秤にかけながら**対処しなければなりません。

　バイデン政権は過去のどの政権よりも、矛盾と混乱をはらんだ外交内政の複雑な課題を突きつけられているのです。

第2章

ホワイトハウス

Key word

COMPROMISE　妥協、譲歩

　「相反する二者が互いの主張する条件に歩み寄って一致点を見出すこと」を表します。日本語だと不本意なニュアンスが含まれる場合もありますが、元は語源の「com（共に）＋promise（約束する）」から「仲裁に従うことを互いに約束する」という意味です。

　本文ではウクライナに侵攻したロシアに対処するべく、アメリカがこれまで批判してきた国々への外交姿勢の転換を余儀なくされたことを解説しています。ロシアと欧米との石油をめぐる攻防に、人権問題などによって距離を置いてきたサウジアラビアとの関係改善や、同じく人権問題を抱えるトルコが北欧2国のNATO加盟申請を承認した際の賞賛など、「不本意な」妥協を強いられています。

例文

The agreement was a product of compromise between the two governments.
その合意は、両国政府による妥協の産物であった。

There's no room for compromise.
妥協の余地はない。

The scandal compromised his reputation.
そのスキャンダルは彼の名誉を損なうものだった。

 あなたはどう答える？

What is Japan's diplomatic stance?
日本はどのような外交姿勢をとっていますか？

> **ヒント**　戦後の日本は、日米同盟をもとにした安全保障、自由主義諸国との国際協調、アジアの一員として各国と経済連携協定を締結するなどして、世界との関係を維持しています。

覚えておくと便利な単語、表現

- [ ] based on the foundation of the Japan-US alliance　日米同盟を基礎に
- [ ] economic partnership agreement [EPA]　経済連携協定
- [ ] value international cooperation　国際協調を重視する

第8話
タリバンのアフガニスタン制圧が
もたらす影響

Article 8
Impacts of the Taliban on Afghanistan
and the World

US drafts airlines to support Afghan evacuation. UK Prime minister Boris Johnson has said he will bring G7 leaders together for urgent talks on the situation in Afghanistan on Tuesday.

—— BBC

（アメリカはアフガンからの人員退去のための航空機を航空会社から調達。イギリスのボリス・ジョンソン首相は、アフガン情勢についてG7緊急会議を火曜日に招集）

The Islamist Taliban's **seizure** of Kabul shocked the world.

Those who know the region well criticize the US and other Western countries for imposing their own values on Afghanistan in an attempt to promote democracy **without taking into account** the local culture, ethnicity, and customs, which may have contributed to the animosity among the Afghan people.

China's position is also delicate. It has been criticized internationally for persecuting the Uighurs, a predominantly Muslim population, so it was wary that some of them might join Islamic **extremists** via Afghanistan. Therefore, when the Taliban brought down the **US-leaning** government, China immediately tried to establish friendly relations with Afghanistan. By doing so, it hopes that it may be able to persuade Afghanistan to **expel** Uighur extremists.

What about India? This change in Afghanistan posed a direct military threat to India, since Pakistan, which is at odds with the Hindu nation of India, also **harbors** Islamic extremists hostile to them.

No one in the West ever expected that Afghanistan would be **overwhelmed** by the Taliban so suddenly. Its strategy appears very similar to that of Mao Zedong before the war in China. When Mao was engaged in fierce fighting with the Kuomintang and Japanese forces, he focused on expanding his power in **rural areas**. He attacked landlords and gave their lands away to peasants, causing the peasants to blindly support him. As a result, it became easier to **manipulate public opinion** and eventually unify China.

▶ extremist ➔ p.86

イスラム勢力タリバンのカブール**制圧**は世界に衝撃を
与えました。

現地をよく知る人は、アメリカをはじめ西側諸国が民
主化を進めるにあたって、アフガニスタンに自らの価値
観を押し付け、現地の文化や民族性、さらには風習に**寄
り添わなかった**ことが、人々の反感につながったのでは
ないかと批判します。

中国の立場も微妙です。イスラム教徒の多いウイグル
人を迫害していると世界から批判を受けている中国は、
ウイグル人の一部がアフガニスタンを経由してイスラム
過激派と合流することを警戒していました。そこで中国
は、タリバンが**アメリカ寄り**の政権を崩壊させたとき、即
座にアフガニスタンとの友好関係の樹立を試みました。
そのことによって、ウイグルの過激派たちをアフガニス
タンから**退去させる**糸口となることを期待しているのか
もしれません。

インドはどうでしょう。ヒンドゥー教国家インドと対
立するパキスタンには、彼らに敵対的なイスラム過激派
が**潜伏している**ため、今回のアフガニスタンの変化は、イ
ンドにとって直接の軍事的脅威となりました。

そもそも、こうも急にアフガニスタンがタリバンに**席
巻される**とは、欧米の誰も予測していませんでした。タ
リバンの行動は戦前の毛沢東の戦略によく似ています。
国民党や日本軍と激烈な戦闘を展開していたころの毛沢
東は、**農村**での勢力拡大に注力しました。地主を攻撃し、
奪った土地を小作農に与え、農民の盲目的な支持を取り
付けたのです。その結果、**世論操作**が容易になり、最終
的には中国を統一できたのです。

▶タリバンはイスラム教神
学校マドラサの学生が中心
となって結成されたスンニ
派組織。イスラム法に基づ
き「アフガニスタン・イスラ
ム首長国」として統治する
ことを目的に、敵対組織や
駐留外国軍を攻撃対象とし
てきた。

第2章

The same was true of the Taliban. They, too, distributed wealth in rural areas and accepted rural soldiers who had surrendered from government forces. In addition, they acquired **state-of-the-art** US military weapons through guerrilla warfare. The US attempted to suppress urban areas as the wealthy kept their assets in cities, and educated people also gathered in those areas. Interacting with them and gaining their support gave them optimism that Afghanistan would become the democratic state the US wanted it to be. However, the Taliban's rural strategy was a brilliant way to **undermine** these efforts.

Another mistake the US made was related to Japan. When it brought Japan to its knees and occupied the country after World War II, it implemented thorough democratization in order to make Japan a **stronghold** in East Asia. As a result, Japan was transformed from a militaristic nation into a democratic state, becoming a quiet **star pupil** under the US's influence. The occupation of Japan was the most successful investment the US ever made. However, when this approach was applied to Vietnam and Iraq, it failed miserably. This time, 20 years of investment in Afghanistan have **gone to waste.**

In the case of Japan, even though the country was war-torn, it already had usable infrastructure, science and technology, and a literate population. Moreover, most of the ground warfare took place outside the Japanese mainland, and the country had been damaged only by airstrikes. Instead, it was the Japanese army, which had invaded China and other countries, that had suffered.

Unable to move on from the initial experience of successful democratization in Japan, the US tried the same strategies in

　タリバンも同様でした。彼らも農村で富を分配し、政府軍から投降する農村出身の兵士も受け入れました。さらにタリバンは兵士だけではなく、ゲリラ戦によってアメリカ軍の**最新式**の兵器まで獲得したのです。アメリカは都市部を抑えていました。都市部には富裕層が資産を持ち、そこには教育を受けた人々も集まっています。彼らと交流し、彼らの支持を得たことで、アフガニスタンはアメリカの望む民主国家となるはずだと楽観したのです。しかし、タリバンの農村戦略はこうしたアメリカの尽力を**台無し**にするほど見事なものでした。

　もう一つ、アメリカには、日本に関係した誤算がありました。第二次世界大戦で日本を屈服させ占領したとき、アメリカは日本を東アジアの**拠点**とするために、徹底した民主化を実施しました。その結果、日本は軍国主義国家から民主主義国家へと変貌し、見事にア

メリカ傘下の物言わぬ**優等生**となりました。アメリカが行った中で最も成功した投資が、日本の占領だったのです。しかし、このモデルをベトナムでもイラクでも応用したとき、見事に失敗しました。そして今回、アフガニスタンでも20年にわたる投資が**無駄になった**のです。

　日本の場合は戦災を受けていたとはいえ、国内にすでに使用可能なインフラや科学技術、識字率の高い国民がいました。かつ、地上戦のほとんどは日本本土の外で行われ、国内は空爆のみで壊滅させました。他国に侵入し苦しんだのは、実は中国などに進攻していた日本軍だったのです。

　ですから、日本での民主化モデルの成功体験から離れられなかったアメリカは、結果としてベトナムでも、中

第2章

Vietnam, the Middle East, and Central Asia. However, its forces **encountered resistance** from the people due to the completely different circumstances in these countries.

The fall of Afghanistan is deeply rooted in the policies of the Bush administration immediately after the 9/11 terrorist attacks in 2001. President Bush, pushed by the new conservatives known as "neoconservatives," invaded both Afghanistan and Iraq in an attempt to expand US interests in the region. This was met with strong resistance and led to acts of terrorism by IS and other groups. The Biden administration then shifted from the Republican administration's US-centered **policy of unilateral action** to a policy of trying to solve foreign policy problems through **international cooperation** in partnership with other countries. The fall of Afghanistan occurred immediately after this change of direction. The US lost its influence in the region, leaving its allies embarrassed and puzzled.

A senior US military official pointed out that many Asian countries will also pursue their own **military expansion** as they see the US losing its presence in Asia and the Middle East and perceive the danger of Taiwan and Japan relying solely on the US, under the threat of China's expansion of hegemony. This is a threat to stability for all citizens of the world.

The Taliban emphasizes that it is not a group of former Islamic extremists. However, while it claims to recognize women's rights, it has expressed the condition that it does so "within the principles of Islamic law," and there have been reports of numerous **human rights abuses** against females. Reports are circulating that **persecution** of the people who formerly held power by Taliban members is taking place in the areas under their control, even though they swore not to harm those who

東や中央アジアでも同じことを試みたものの、日本とはまったく違う環境の中で人々の**抵抗に遭遇した**のです。

　アフガニスタンの陥落は、2001年の同時多発テロ直後のブッシュ政権の政策に遠因があります。ブッシュ大統領はネオコン（新保守主義）という新しい保守派の人々に押され、アメリカの権益を拡大しようとアフガニスタンとイラクの双方に侵攻しました。これが泥沼の抵抗に遭い、ISなどによるテロ行為にもつながりました。そしてバイデン政権は、共和党政権によるアメリカ中心の**単独行動主義の政策**から、他国と連携した**国際協調**によって外交問題の解決に挑む政策へと転換しました。アフガニスタンの陥落は、そうした方向転換の直後に起きた事件です。そして、アメリカはこの地域への影響力を失い、アメリカの同盟国も当惑します。

　あるアメリカ軍の幹部は、アジアや中東でのプレゼンスを失いつつあるアメリカを見て、中国の覇権拡張の脅威にさらされる台湾や日本がアメリカのみに依存する危険性を察知し、アジアの多くの国も独自に**軍備拡張**を進めるのではないかと指摘します。これは世界市民すべてが抱く安定への脅威です。
　タリバンは、自らが以前のイスラム過激派の集団ではないと強調します。しかし、女性の権利も認めるとは言いながら、「イスラム法の原則の中で」という条件を表明し、女性に対する多くの**人権侵害**が報告されています。アメリカへの協力者にも危害は加えないと言いながら、支配地域では旧勢力への**迫害**が進んでいるという報道も飛び交います。再び政権を掌握したタリバンがどう国際社会とつながってゆくかを見極めるのは時期尚早なのです。

▶ネオコンとは自由主義や民主主義を基盤とする体制を堅持し、保守主義的な社会福祉や富の分配には干渉しないという、特に米国で顕著な政治思想。国防・安全保障の重視、キリスト教信仰の強化なども特徴の一つである。

第2章

had cooperated with the US. It is too early to see how the Taliban will connect with the international community now that they have gained political power again.

We should note that the Taliban is not a **monolithic** group, as it is divided into various internal factions, including **radicals** and **moderates**. History has shown that revolutions often create room for new **internal conflicts** that take a considerable amount of time to settle down. The world is now watching, holding its breath, to see how the major powers will deal with this new Islamic movement.

　実際、タリバンの中にも**急進派**や**穏健派**など様々な分派がいて、**一枚岩**ではありません。革命は常に新たな**内部抗争**を生み、左右に揺れながら落ち着くまで相当の時間を要することは、歴史が物語っています。今、主要国がこの新たなイスラム圏での動きにどのように対処するか、世界が見つめているのです。

第2章

Key word

EXTREMIST 過激派、過激主義者

　「〔方法やものの見方が〕過激な、極端な人・グループ」を表します。中東問題がクローズアップされる際に、「イスラム過激派（Islamic extremist）」としてこの言葉がよく使われます。彼らはイスラムの理想社会を実現するためであれば殺人や暴力も辞さないのです。同じような文脈で「イスラム原理主義者（Islamic fundamentalist）」という言葉もでてきますが、このfundamentalistはどの宗教においても、その原理に対して頑迷な人々のことを指しています。同様に「過激派、急進主義者」を表すradicalという言葉は、「〔改革が〕抜本的な」「〔変化が〕革命的な」といった根本から覆すような意味でも使われます。

例文

The extremist group carried out a series of violent attacks against the government.
過激派組織は、政府に対して一連の激しい攻撃を行った。

There are numerous fundamentalist Islamic groups throughout the world.
世界には数えきれないほど多くのイスラム原理主義者の集団がいる。

She has radical opinions on education.
彼女は教育に関して急進的な意見を持っている。

 あなたはどう答える？

How much military power does Japan have?
日本にはどのくらいの軍事力がありますか？

ヒント　日本は防衛費をGDP比４％まで引き上げようとしています。アメリカや国産の最新鋭装備もあり軍事力は高いといえます。ただ、自衛隊員は約24万人と諸外国と比べて少ないです。

 覚えておくと便利な単語、表現

☐ defense spending as a percentage of GDP　対GDP比での防衛費
☐ Japan Self-Defense Forces　自衛隊
☐ state-of-the-art military weapons　最新式の兵器

第9話
深刻化する米中対立とネット世界

Article 9
The Ever-Growing US-China Feud
and the Online World

"That stronger hand threatens Hong Kong's future as a global commercial hub, but business leaders increasingly fear resisting a Chinese government that does not tolerate dissent."

—— New York Times

（世界経済のハブとしての香港の将来が大きな脅威にさらされる中、ビジネスリーダーたちは中国政府の強硬で頑なな態度にどう向き合うか神経を尖らせている）

It is said that our era is an era of struggle between the "**author-itarianism**" that China and Russia are best known for, and the "**democracy**" that is common in the West and other areas.

In particular, the conflict between the US and China was the focus of the world's attention until Russia invaded Ukraine.

As the US transitioned from the Republican Party's Trump administration to the Democratic Party's Biden administration, the rift with China deepened even further. Following **friction** over trade issues and the entry of telecommunications equipment-related companies such as Huawei into the US market, America has consistently condemned China and strengthened economic sanctions over its suppression of the democracy movement in Hong Kong and **human rights issues** for ethnic minorities, such as the Uighur people. Of course, the US is also sensitive to issues such as China's **maritime expansion** into the South China Sea and maintaining Taiwan's independence.

Nevertheless, with the economic crisis caused by the coronavirus and the urgent need to rebuild the US economy, it is uncertain how far the two countries can go in confronting each other. It is also the US's intention to have China somehow **remain neutral** on the issue of Russia's Ukraine problem.

But what about China's point of view?

It is obvious to everyone that the Chinese government will be criticized if it suppresses the democracy movement in Hong Kong and forces ethnic minorities to become Chinese. However, China must have determined that there would be no **thaw** in its relations with the US under the Biden administration. Although various negotiations are possible on the issue of trade friction, human rights issues in China and hegemony issues in East Asia

▶ democracy → p.94

第2章

　我々の時代は、中国やロシアをはじめとする「**権威主義**」と欧米を中心とする「**民主主義**」との闘いの時代であると言われています。

　特に、ロシアがウクライナに侵攻するまでは、アメリカと中国との対立が世界の注目を集めていました。

　実は、アメリカは共和党のトランプ政権から民主党のバイデン政権に変わったあと、中国との溝がさらに深まっています。貿易問題、ファーウェイなどの通信機器関連の米国進出をめぐる**摩擦**に続き、香港での民主化運動の抑圧への対処、ウイグル族など少数民族に対する**人権問題**などをめぐって、アメリカは一貫して中国を非難し、経済制裁を強めてきました。もちろん南シナ海への中国の**海洋進出**や台湾の独立をどのように維持するかという課題にも、アメリカは神経を尖らせています。

　とはいえ、コロナウイルスでの景気後退もあり、アメリカ経済の立て直しという急務がある中で、どこまでアメリカと中国とが対立してゆくかは不透明なはずです。ロシアのウクライナ問題ではなんとか中国に**中立を保って**もらいたいというのもアメリカの本音です。

　では、中国から見ればどうでしょうか。

　香港の民主化運動を弾圧し、少数民族の中国化を強行すれば、中国政府が非難されることは誰が見ても明らかです。しかし中国は、人権問題を旗印にトランプ前大統領を破ったバイデン政権下では、アメリカとの**雪解け**はないものと判断しているはずです。貿易摩擦の問題は様々な交渉が可能でしょう。しかし、中国での人権問題や東アジアにおける覇権問題は、バイデン政権でも両国にと

will probably remain non-negotiable for both countries. That is why China wanted to implement policies to firmly protect its own interests while the US **had its hands full** with the pandemic.

As a matter of fact, China probably wanted to avoid causing riots in Hong Kong. As the country embraces capitalism, it would not have wanted to make waves in Hong Kong, which was originally a **free economy** with many assets flowing in from overseas. However, when attempts were made to unite Hong Kong and China, China was hit with an unexpected wave of protests. In the background must have been China's overconfidence in the **pro-China sentiment** within Hong Kong. Also, at that time, there was a growing wave of opposition to the Tsai administration in Taiwan, led by Han Kuo-yu and others, and a push for economic **accommodation** with China. This situation was another reason for Beijing's misjudgment.

However, if China had given in to the protests that erupted in Hong Kong and elsewhere, the Xi Jinping administration would have lost face, and its base of power would have been shaken. Even if China realizes that it has reacted hastily to Hong Kong, too much damage has already been done for it to repair matters.

Furthermore, the Hong Kong issue has made Taiwan more cautious, and Tsai Ing-wen has been **reelected**.

China, for its part, could not back down, having no choice but to stand face-to-face with the US.

One more thing that should be taken into account is telecommunication devices and social media.

The US is highly concerned that Chinese social media and communication software will be utilized to influence public opinion, and for **intelligence operations**. Furthermore, the US

って譲れない課題として残るはずです。であれば、中国としてはアメリカがコロナ問題で**手一杯**のうちに、自国の利益をしっかりと守る政策を実施したいと思っていたはずです。

　実は、中国も本音では、香港での騒動は起こしたくなかったのではないでしょうか。中国自体が、資本主義経済を受け入れている以上、元々**自由経済**の中で海外から多くの資産が流入していた香港で波風は立てたくなかったはずです。しかし、香港を中国と一体化しようと試みたとき、中国は予想を上回る抗議の渦に見舞われました。背景には、香港内の**親中意識**への中国の過信があったはずです。また、台湾でもその当時、韓国瑜氏などを中心に、蔡英文政権に反対し、経済的にも中国との**融和策**を進める波が高まっていました。この状況も北京が判断を誤った原因でした。

　しかし、香港などで沸き起こった抗議に屈してしまえば、習近平政権にとっては面子が丸つぶれとなり、政権基盤が揺らいでしまいます。中国は、香港への対応を急ぎすぎたことに内心気付いていたとしても、引き返すにはすでにいろいろなことが起こりすぎてしまいました。

　さらに、香港問題で台湾が警戒心を強め、蔡英文氏が**再選**されてしまいます。

　中国としても、振り上げた拳が下ろせないまま、アメリカと睨み合わざるを得なくなったわけです。

　そこで注目したいのは、もう一つの火種である通信機器とSNSの問題です。

　アメリカは、中国で開発されたSNSや通信ソフトが、中国の世論誘導や**諜報活動**に使われることを強く警戒しています。さらに、AIと通信技術の双方において、アメ

▶アメリカでは、中国のテクノロジー企業が運営する動画共有サービス「TikTok」の利用を規制する動きが相次いでおり、連邦政府が関係する端末や州政府が所有する機器、ネットワーク上での利用が次々と禁止されている。

and China are **in fierce competition** for a larger share of the AI and communications software market.

In fact, after sanctions were imposed on China's semiconductor trade and other activities, the global distribution of semiconductors changed dramatically, forcing a restructuring of the **distribution network**. In the latter half of the 20th century, the **nuclear arms race** was a symbol of the Cold War, and as a by-product of that, the advance into space fueled the confrontation between the US and the Soviet Union. Today, the competition for a share of the telecommunications software market has replaced nuclear weapons to become the biggest challenge of the Cold War between the US and China.

China is beginning to show extreme dislike of foreign influence over its own education, as seen in its attempts to curb English learning. Furthermore, the world is watching how Japan, South Korea, and Taiwan will respond to China's new moves. There is also concern regarding how China's actions will affect North Korea, which is known for its repeated **missile launches**. From China's point of view, it may be convenient that the Far East is divided due to political conflicts between Japan and South Korea.

As the game being played by the US and China continues in the future, our home in the Far East is the region that is most likely to be **at its mercy**.

リカと中国はそのシェアの拡大をめぐり、**熾烈な競争を展開しています。**

　実際、中国への半導体貿易等への制裁のあと、世界の半導体の流通は大きく変化し、**流通網の再編を余儀なく**されました。20世紀後半は、冷戦の象徴といえば**核の拡散競争**で、その副産物として宇宙への進出が米ソの対立を煽っていました。現在は、通信ソフトのシェアをめぐる競争こそが、核に代わる米中冷戦の最大の課題となっているのです。

　今、中国は英語教育を抑制しているように、自国の教育に海外が影響を与えることを極度に嫌い始めています。さらに日本や韓国、そして台湾が中国の新たな動きにどう対応するか、世界が注目しています。**ミサイルの発射**を繰り返す北朝鮮に中国がどう影響するかも気になるところです。中国からしてみれば、日韓の政治対立などで極東が一枚岩にならないことは、都合が良いのかもしれません。

　これからも続くことが予測されるアメリカと中国との様々な駆け引きの中で、最も**翻弄され**そうなのが、我々の住む極東地域に他ならないのです。

Key word

DEMOCRACY 民主主義、民主制

　人民・民衆が国または地域の権力を所有し、それを自ら行使する政治思想または政治体制のことを指します。対義語は本文にもでてきた「権威主義（authoritarianism）」で、権力を元首または政治組織が独占して統治を行う政治思想または政治体制のことです。これがさらに極端になると「全体主義（totalitarianism）」として、個人の権利や思想は国家の利害と一致するように統制されます。

　語源は古代ギリシア語の「デーモクラティア（人民権力・民衆支配）」ですが、世界で最初に標榜した古代ギリシア（アテナイ）の「デモクラシー」はのちに失敗し「衆愚政治」と揶揄する言葉として使われるようになったそうです。

....

例文

Japan has adopted an indirect democracy.
日本は間接民主制を採用している。

The West is opposed to authoritarianism.
欧米は権威主義に反対している。

The first totalitarian state in the world was Italy under the Mussolini regime.
世界で最初の全体主義国家は、ムッソリーニ政権下のイタリアだ。

 あなたはどう答える？

How will US-China friction affect Japan?
米中摩擦は日本にどのような影響をもたらしますか？

> **ヒント** 中国は日本にとって最大の貿易相手国で、日系企業の海外拠点数は最多です。米国は安全保障上の同盟国であり、日本は世界最大の対米投資国で現地の雇用を創出しています。

覚えておくと便利な単語、表現

- ☐ **create jobs** 雇用を創出する
- ☐ **Japan's principal trading partner** 日本の主要な貿易相手国
- ☐ **Japanese-affiliated company** 日系企業

第10話
ポピュリズムの政策に翻弄された世界の実情

Article 10
The Realities of a World at the Mercy of Populist Policies

Several recent attacks have not been charged as hate crimes, fueling protests and outrage among many Asian Americans.

—— New York Times

（最近の暴行がヘイトクライムとみなされないことに、多くのアジア系アメリカ人は怒りを感じ、抗議をしている）

During the Coronavirus pandemic, **hate crimes** against Asian Americans became an issue in the US. Many point out that this is a negative legacy brought about by **populism.**

When interpreting international politics, we need to be aware of the interests and objectives among nations that lie beyond the messages being exchanged on the surface. It is no exaggeration to say that it is always a matter of **deciphering the true intentions** behind the messages of professional politicians and bureaucrats.

One way to understand the problem of populism is through the idea of **universal harmony.** This is a concept proposed by Early Modern philosophers and others that all seemingly unrelated things are in fact firmly in harmony with the will of God. Modern history has **made great progress** by applying this idea of universal harmony to international politics.

For example, until the Middle Ages, wars consisted of repeated mass **slaughters** and **lootings.** In the Early Modern period, however, war became the ultimate means of **diplomatic negotiation**, with the victor and the vanquished finally negotiating, setting **terms of surrender**, and protecting the sovereignty of the vanquished. The winner leaves the losing side with an organization and representatives to negotiate and discuss terms.

This idea was first realized in 1648 under the Treaty of Westphalia at the end of the Thirty Years' War, a conflict that had engulfed the whole of Europe. The treaty has been hailed as the world's first **multilateral treaty**. Since then, all diplomacy in Europe and the US has proceeded with negotiations involving compromise, with an implicit awareness of the supreme goal of

▶ populism ➙ p.102

コロナが蔓延する中、アメリカでアジア系への**ヘイト
クライム**が問題となりました。それは、**ポピュリズム**が
生み出した負の遺産ではないのかと多くの人は指摘しま
す。

国際政治を読み解くとき、我々は表面で交わされてい
るメッセージの向こうにある、国家間の利害や目的を意
識する必要があります。それは常にプロの政治家や官僚
によって設定された、表面に現れるメッセージの**真意を
読み解く**ことだといっても過言ではありません。

ポピュリズムの問題を理解する一つの方法として、
「**予定調和**」という考え方があります。予定調和とは、一
見すると無関係なすべてのものが、実はしっかりと神
の意志と調和しているという近世の哲学者などによって
提唱された概念です。近代史は国際政治にこの予定調和
という考え方を当てはめることで**大きく進歩してきまし
た**。

「予定調和説」を提唱したド
イツの哲学者ライプニッツ

例えば、中世までは戦争は徹底した**殺戮**と**略奪**のくり
返しでした。しかし、そんな殺戮への反省から、近代で
は戦争ですら**外交交渉**における究極の手段となり、勝者
と敗者とは最終的に交渉をし、**降伏条件**を決め、敗者の
主権も守られるようになりました。勝者は敗者側に、交
渉のための組織や代表を残存させ、条件を話し合うので
す。

1648年、三十年戦争といわれたヨーロッパ全体を巻き
込んだ戦争が終結したときに、この考え方がウェストフ
ァリア条約という名前で初めて実現したと言われていま
す。この条約は世界初の**多国間条約**として評価されまし
た。以来、欧米での外交は、すべて最終的なゴールを暗
に意識しながら、着地点を巡った交渉を進めるようにな

▶三十年戦争は主にドイツ
（神聖ローマ帝国）を舞台
に、1618年から1648年にか
けて戦われた国際的戦争。
プロテスタントとカトリッ
クの対立やハプスブルク家
とブルボン家の抗争など、
宗教的・政治的な側面があ
った。

第2章

compromise. The concept of universal harmony in God's world also came to function in conflicts of human interests. However, the **cunning gamesmanship** of diplomats and bureaucrats has been essential to this practice.

But the complex threads of universal harmony gradually became tangled, and the world seemed to have lost its balance, even though nations were still working for universal harmony. The situation led to World War I, and was followed by the rise of fascism, which led to World War II. With these two waves, the previous system collapsed, and people sought a new way to strike a balance in international relations.

A new order also requires principles. These principles led to respect for **basic human rights**, the elimination of **racial discrimination**, and the concept of respect for **national sovereignty**. This was the basis for the common diplomatic practice in the West from the Cold War era to the present. Legal nations have further developed a variety of know-how so that they can protect each other's ultimate interests through international law.

However, countries such as Japan, which have newly entered the international scene, are sometimes **at the mercy of** this traditional Western diplomatic philosophy. In fact, it is safe to say that this know-how is essential wisdom for becoming a professional politician. It is necessary to take a fighting stance and stare each other down, while looking for a point of compromise.

However, the world of professional politicians, which is premised on universal harmony, **alienates** the general public. The separation of awareness and information between the professional world and the non-professional world makes alienation more serious, and people fall into **distrust of politics**.

ったわけです。神の世界の予定調和という概念が、人類
の利害の対立でも機能するようになったのです。ただ、こ
の実践には、外交官や官僚たちの**老獪な駆け引き**が必要
不可欠でした。

　しかし、各国がそんな予定調和のために努力している
にもかかわらず、複雑に張り巡らされた糸は次第にもつ
れ、世界はバランスを失ったかのように見えました。そ
して第一次世界大戦が起こり、その後に勃興したファシ
ズムによって、第二次世界大戦につながりました。この2
つの波で、それまでの体制は崩壊し、人々は国際関係の
中で新たなバランスのとり方を模索したのです。

　新たな秩序には原則も必要です。その原則が**基本的人
権**を尊重すること、**人種差別**を撤廃すること、さらには
国家主権の尊重の概念へとつながりました。これが、冷
戦時代から現在に至る欧米での外交上の常識を構築した
のです。法治国家同士が、さらに国際法によってお互い
の究極の利益を保護できるように、様々なノウハウを培
ってきたのです。

　とはいえ、この欧米の伝統的な外交哲学に、日本など
他の地域から新たに参入した国家は、時には**翻弄されて**
しまいます。実際にこのノウハウは、プロの政治家にな
るために必須の知恵であるといっても差し支えありませ
ん。拳を振り上げながら、常にお互いが落とし所を探っ
ていることを知っている、という冷静に見つめ合う駆け
引きが求められるのです。

　しかし、この予定調和を前提にしたプロの世界は、一
般の市民との間に**疎外を生んで**しまいます。プロの世界
とそうでない世界との意識や情報の隔絶が、疎外をより
深刻にし、人々は**政治不信**に陥ります。

第2章

When distrust becomes more serious, people will be swept away by populism and universal harmony will not work. Hitler and the now problematic Russian president Putin became **dictators** using such popular psychology. What populist leaders have in common is extreme behavior that is unpredictable in the world of normal politics. When such leaders **dare to destroy** the universal harmony of professional politicians, citizens **vent their anger** and applaud. For example, when former President Trump called the coronavirus the "China virus," intentionally ignoring a line that politicians who value universal harmony cannot cross, people said, "Well spoken," and it seems to have contributed to the rise in hate crimes directed at people of Asian descent.

And when populism began to interfere with universal harmony, it became a factor that allowed Russia to build public support for the invasion of Ukraine.

Some people say that the history of humankind is a history of the **division of labor**. The more complex a society becomes, the less it can be sustained by individual competence, and the more essential it becomes to have a professional workforce. Ironically, domestic politics and international politics have also become a business for professionals to manage. The disparity in awareness between professionals and ordinary citizens is a **breeding ground** for distrust and populism.

　不信がさらに深刻になったとき、人々はポピュリズム
に流され、予定調和が機能しなくなるのです。ヒトラー
や、現在問題となっているロシアのプーチン大統領が、そ
んな大衆心理を利用した**独裁者**となるわけです。ポピュ
リズムの指導者に共通していることは、通常の政治の世
界では予測されない極端な言動にあります。プロの政治
家による予定調和を**あえて破壊する**ことで、市民は**鬱憤
を晴らし**、喝采を送るのです。例えば、予定調和を重ん
ずる政治家が越えられない一線を意図的に
無視して、トランプ前大統領がコロナウイ
ルスを「チャイナウイルス」と呼んだこと
で、人々が「よくぞ言ってくれました」と
歓迎し、それがアジア系の人々に向けられ
たヘイトクライムの一因となったのです。

　そしてポピュリズムが予定調和を阻害す
るようになると、ロシアが国民の支持を集
めてウクライナ侵攻に向かう要因となったのです。

　人類の歴史は、**分業の歴史**だといわれています。社会が
複雑になればなるほど、個人の能力では社会を維持でき
なくなり、専門職が必要不可欠になってしまいます。皮
肉なことに、国内政治も国際政治も専門職が管理する業
務となってしまいました。そこで生まれる市民との意識
格差が不信感とポピュリズムの**温床**になるわけです。

POPULISM　ポピュリズム、大衆（迎合）主義

　支配階級や知識人といった「エリート」と「一般大衆」を対比させたうえで、大衆側の権利こそ尊重されるべきだと主張する政治思想を表します。一定の見識があり合理的な判断ができるエリート層よりも、一時的な感情や空気によって政治的態度を決めてしまう大衆の意思を重視し、扇動するような急進的政策を訴えて政治的基盤をつくりあげる手法を指すことが多いです。もとは19世紀末のアメリカで結党された人民党（ポピュリスト党）の政治運動によって広まった言葉だとされています。最近ではドナルド・トランプ前米大統領の登場によって、この言葉が注目されるようになりました。

例文

Fascism in Italy and Nazism in Germany are also considered a form of populism.
イタリアのファシズムやドイツのナチズムもポピュリズムの一種とされている。

We need to be skeptical of words and information to avoid getting caught up in populism.
ポピュリズムに踊らされないよう、言葉や情報に対して懐疑的になる必要があるのだ。

I fear that nationalism and populism will increase globally.
ナショナリズムやポピュリズムが世界的に高まることを危惧しています。

あなたはどう答える？

Is there a problem with hate crimes in Japan?
日本でヘイトクライムが問題になることはありますか？

ヒント　在日韓国・朝鮮人に対する過激なデモを契機に「ヘイトスピーチ解消法」が2016年に施行されました。しかし、日本における実態調査や状況把握は未だに行われていません。

覚えておくと便利な単語、表現

- [ ] **eliminate racial discrimination**　人種差別を撤廃する
- [ ] **freedom of thought and expression**　思想と表現の自由
- [ ] **Hate Speech Act of 2016**　ヘイトスピーチ解消法

第3章

複雑化・多様化する国際社会

Chapter 3

An Increasingly Complex and Diverse International Society

第11話
カリブ系のアーバンポップスが象徴する
アメリカの世情

Article 11
America as Symbolized
by Caribbean Urban Pop Music

Miami is nicknamed the "Capital of Latin America" because of its high population of Spanish-speakers.
—— Wikipedia

（マイアミは「ラテンアメリカの都」と呼ばれるほどにスペイン語を話す人が多い）

What will society look like after fully recovering from the pandemic? This is a theme of discussion around the world. To help **predict** what may actually happen, let's take a look at the current state of the music industry in Miami. Caribbean music is very popular in the area right now.

It is incredibly **diverse**, including genres such as salsa and reggae. Now that these particular music styles are merging together in Miami, a new musical phenomenon is taking shape. Latin urban pop is beginning to spread from Miami to other parts of the country.

A lot has happened in South and Central America over the past few years. For starters, **political conflict** has continued in Venezuela, where the people have been suffering from food shortages. The coronavirus has also **taken a toll on the economy** and the Caribbean has recently experienced a major hurricane. Both Miami and New York City are now the gateways for Caribbean and Latin American immigrants.

Many of these immigrants happen to be musicians. Some live as buskers, collecting coins from passersby in places like the New York City subway. Despite having huge talent, their lives are not easy. Most unfortunately for them, the pandemic has struck, causing people to **disappear** from the streets and live music venues.

Many people from Puerto Rico, a US territory in the Caribbean, have immigrated to the US mainland since the 1920s. Now having full American **citizenship**, some of these immigrants work as active musicians, and they too have been severely

コロナパンデミック後の社会がどのようになるのか。これは世界共通のテーマでしょう。そのことを**予測する**一つのヒントとして、マイアミでの音楽活動にスポットを当ててみます。マイアミでは今カリブ系の音楽が盛んです。

マイアミのビーチ

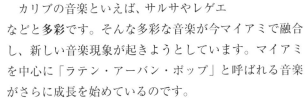

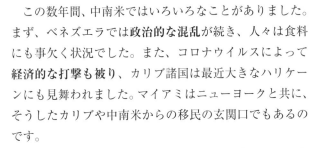

カリブの音楽といえば、サルサやレゲエなどと**多彩**です。そんな多彩な音楽が今マイアミで融合し、新しい音楽現象が起きようとしています。マイアミを中心に「ラテン・アーバン・ポップ」と呼ばれる音楽がさらに成長を始めているのです。

この数年間、中南米ではいろいろなことがありました。まず、ベネズエラでは**政治的な混乱**が続き、人々は食料にも事欠く状況でした。また、コロナウイルスによって**経済的な打撃も被り**、カリブ諸国は最近大きなハリケーンにも見舞われました。マイアミはニューヨークと共に、そうしたカリブや中南米からの移民の玄関口でもあるのです。

移民の中には、多くのミュージシャンも含まれていました。彼らは時にストリートミュージシャンとして、例えばニューヨークの地下鉄コンコースを行き来する人々からコインを集めて生活します。才能はありながらも、生活は決して楽ではありません。そこに、今回のパンデミックが襲いかかり、人々が街から、ライブハウスから**姿を消した**のです。

特にカリブ海の中でもアメリカの自治領となっているプエルトリコからは、1920年代から多くの人々がアメリカ本土に移住し、アメリカの**市民権**をもって生活しています。そうした人々の中にもミュージシャンとして活動

▶ここでいう自治領とはアメリカ主権下の属領もしくは保護領で、自治政府による内政は認められるが国防や外交はアメリカが行う。住民はアメリカ国籍を持つが所得税の納税義務はなく、大統領選挙への投票権は持たない。

第3章

affected by the pandemic.

They moved from all over the US to Miami, which was originally populated by many Cuban immigrants. They spoke Spanish fluently and were familiar with Latin culture. Musicians from the Caribbean and surrounding areas began to **exchange ideas** and collaborate with each other in Miami.

Miami is located in Florida, which is one of the so-called "Red States," where the Republican Party **won majorities** in the 2020 presidential elections. Northern Florida, also known as an area that votes Republican, is said to be the most **conservative** region in the US. However, many people from New York and other urban areas would rather move to the southern part of the state to spend their retirement in a warmer climate.

There, new people from the Caribbean are also pouring into cities such as Miami. The music movement symbolizes this transition from a conservative to a liberal environment.

Not only are the people relatively new to the US but many of them are also legitimate American voters who started out in urban areas many years ago and then moved to Miami's mainly Hispanic community.

Republicans are now most concerned about the transfer of voters from other urban areas into previous Republican **strongholds** like Florida. The pandemic is one of the major factors behind the movement of these people. As many of them were encouraged to work from home, they migrated to more-rural cities where people can enjoy a more natural way of life.

▶ conservative → p.112

してきた人がいて、彼らもパンデミックの影響をまともに受けてしまいました。

　そんな彼らが、アメリカの各地からマイアミへと移住してきたのです。マイアミは元々キューバ系の移民も多く、スペイン語も通じやすく、ラテン系の文化への受容性もありました。カリブやその周辺からやってきたミュージシャンは、マイアミでお互いに**情報を交換し**、協力して音楽活動を始めたのです。

　そんなマイアミのあるフロリダ州は、2020年の大統領選挙で共和党が**過半数を取った**、いわゆる「レッドステート」です。共和党の票田とも言われるフロリダ北部は、アメリカでも最も**保守層の多い**地域だと言われています。しかし、マイアミなどの南部の都市部には今ニューヨークなどから、暖かい土地で老後を送ろうと多くの人が移住をしてきています。

　そこに、カリブ諸国から新たな人々が流れ込みます。それを象徴的に表しているのが、このミュージックムーブメントなのです。

　彼らはアメリカにやってきた新参者だけではありません。何年も前からアメリカの都市部で活動を始め、その後マイアミのスペイン語コミュニティに移住してきた、れっきとしたアメリカの有権者も多く含まれています。

　今、共和党は、元々**地盤の強かった**こうした地域へ他の都市部から有権者が流入することを最も警戒しているのです。コロナパンデミックは、そうした人の動きに拍車をかけました。自宅勤務が奨励されるなかで、より自然の豊かな地方都市への人々の移動が加速したのです。

The urban areas of Texas, and the states of Georgia and Arizona, are examples of such new trends in America. There, many areas switched to "blue" in last year's elections as more and more people supported the Democratic Party, which is associated with the color blue. It is often said that the US is a **divided** country, and this resistance to the influx of new populations into the states, which has even begun to affect voter **voting behavior**, is also making the division in people's attitudes more serious.

When we study international affairs, we tend to focus only on what is happening in one region. However, as mentioned here, nations of the world are constantly influencing one another. **Political changes**, economic crises, and natural disasters in the Caribbean are actually related to the new musical activities in Miami.

Of course, this is not a new phenomenon. The spread of cultures through ethnic migrations that occurred in the distant past is now driving people more quickly and creating new human activities in many parts of the world.

This influence is so strong that it is beginning to have a major impact on, for example, the **political map of the US**. Therefore, when we think about post-coronavirus society, we need to consider this global perspective.

　テキサス州の都市部、そして前回の大統領選挙では民主党への支持者が増え「ブルーステート」となったジョージア州やアリゾナ州は、そうしたアメリカの新しい傾向を象徴している事例なのです。よくアメリカが**分断されている**と言われますが、このように、州の中に新たな人口が流入し、それが有権者の**投票行動**にまで影響を与え始めたことへの抵抗感も、人々の意識の分断をより深刻にしているのです。

　国際情勢を見るとき、我々はとかく一つの地域で起きていることだけに注目しがちです。しかし、ここで触れたように、カリブ諸国で起こった**政変**や経済危機、そして自然災害などが、マイアミでの新しい音楽活動の遠因となっている事実が語るように、世界は常に影響し合い、社会を変化させているのです。

　もちろん、これは今に始まったことではありません。遠い昔に起きた民族移動による文化の伝播が、今ではより迅速に人々を駆り立て、世界のあちこちで新しい人の活動を生み出しているのです。

　このことが、例えば**アメリカ政治の勢力地図**の上にも大きな影響を与え始めています。コロナ後の社会を考えるときも、こうしたグローバルな視点に立ってみることが必要なのです。

第3章

Key word

CONSERVATIVE 保守的な

　主義・手法・ファッションスタイルなどで「コンサバ」と略して使われることが多い言葉ですが、政治の世界では liberal（進歩的な）の対立項として使われます。しかし、ある意味で conservative には二つのニュアンスがあるといえます。一つは頑固に物事を変えないでいること。そして、もう一つが過去の蓄積を大切にしながら判断をするという意味合いです。前者は否定的に、後者はどちらかというと肯定的に使用されます。一つの単語の中に、このように二つの価値観がある場合、そのどちらかを選択するためにも、そこに書かれている文脈をきちんと理解する必要があるといえるでしょう。

例文

A conservative tie is preferable to a loud one for a job interview.
面接では派手なネクタイより、地味なネクタイの方が好ましい。

A state with a large conservative population is called a "red state" because the Republican Party is associated with the color red.
共和党のイメージカラーが赤であることから、保守派が多い州を「レッド・ステート」という。

He is financially conservative, but politically liberal.
彼は金銭に関しては保守的だが、政治に関してはリベラルだ。

❓ あなたはどう答える？

Has there been any movement of people in Japan in the face of the coronavirus pandemic?
コロナ禍の日本では人々の移動が起きていますか？

ヒント 　一貫して転入超過だった東京で2020年4月には初めて転出超過となりました。主な行先は近隣3県ですが地方への転出も一定数増加し、地方移住への関心が高まっています。

覚えておくと便利な単語、表現

☐ **encouraged to work from home** 　在宅勤務が奨励される

☐ **excess moving-out[move-in]** 　転出［転入］超過

☐ **take more interest in** 　〜への関心が高まる

第12話
中東の文明へのプライドが生み出す
欧米との確執

Article 12
Pride in Middle Eastern Civilization Sparks Feuds in the West

The greatest tragedy in mankind's entire history may be the hijacking of morality by religion.

—— Arthur Charles Clarke

（人類の歴史を通して最大の悲劇は、宗教が道徳をハイジャックしたことだ）

Article 12

More than 2 million immigrants from the Middle East live in the US. However, many of them criticize American society's **ignorance** of the Arab world. As Americans have become worried about the Middle East, **prejudice** against Muslim immigrants and Islam itself has worsened.

It is important to note that Islamic societies have done a great deal to shape civilizations in the past.

Take Spain, for example. If you look at the Spanish flag, at the bottom of the central emblem, you will see a coat of arms with a pomegranate fruit and leaf. This **symbolizes** the Islamic dynasty that ruled over the southern part of Spain.

In the 8th century, a little over 100 years after the birth of Islam, the Islamic world expanded rapidly, quickly extending its power from North Africa in the west to what is now western China in the east, and expanding its land from the Iberian Peninsula to Europe. Islamic soldiers then invaded France in 732 AD until they were **just barely** stopped at the Battle of Tour Poitiers.

This war took place in Europe during the height of the Middle Ages. Roman Catholicism reigned as the **spiritual pillar** of Western Europe. In order to enhance its own power, church authority suppressed intellectual activities and other religions.

Arthur C. Clarke was a well-known science fiction writer and science expert. He once explained that if the Muslims had won the battle of Tour Poitiers, the history of the **Industrial Revolution** and the subsequent **modernization** it brought would have come

　アメリカでは中東からの200万人以上の移民が生活しています。そんな彼らの多くが批判していることがあります。それはアメリカ社会のアラブ世界に対する**無知**への憤りです。特に中東からのテロをアメリカ人が警戒するようになって以来、イスラム教そのものに加えて、イスラム系移民への**偏見**がひどくなっているのです。

　実際、イスラム社会は過去に文明の形成に多大な功績を残しています。

　話をスペインへと移します。スペインの国旗を見ると、中央の紋章の一番下に、ザクロの実と葉が描かれた紋章があります。それは、スペインの南部一帯を支配していたイスラム王朝を**象徴**したものです。

スペインの国旗

　イスラム教が芽生えて100年少し経った8世紀に、イスラム世界は急速に膨張し、瞬く間に西は北アフリカから東は現在の中国西部にまで勢力を伸ばし、さらにイベリア半島からヨーロッパへと支配地を広げたのです。その勢いは、イスラム教の兵士が西暦732年にフランスに侵入したときに**なんとか**食い止められたほどでした。そのときの戦いをトゥール・ポワティエ間の戦いと言います。

　この戦争があった頃のヨーロッパは中世の真っ只中。ローマ・カトリックが西ヨーロッパの**精神的支柱**として君臨していました。ローマ・カトリックは自らの権威を高めようと、他の宗教や自らの宗旨に反する知的活動を弾圧しました。

　もしトゥール・ポワティエ間の戦いでイスラム側が勝利していれば、**産業革命**やその後の**近代化**の歴史がかなり早まったのではないか、と解説しているイギリス人がいます。SF作家で科学評論家としても知られていた

▶732年にフランス西部のトゥールとポワティエの間で、当時のフランク王国とイスラム帝国のウマイヤ朝との間で起こった戦い。カール・マルテル率いるフランク王国が勝利した。

earlier. This is because much of the civilization that had been developed in the Mediterranean world before the Middle Ages was **preserved** and **cultivated** in the Islamic world. It is said that knowledge from all over the world was kept in books in a library in Baghdad at that time.

Later, 700 years after the Battle of Tour Poitiers, the Renaissance movement began in Europe in an attempt to learn from past civilizations. European academics during the Renaissance learned about a wide variety of subjects from Islamic societies.

Beginning in 1096, Europe organized several **Crusades** against Muslim societies in an attempt to retake the **holy city of Jerusalem**. The conflict between Christian and Muslim societies can be traced back to this point. At the same time, there was a movement in Western Europe aimed at removing Muslims from the Iberian Peninsula and establishing a Christian state. In 1492, the Muslims were expelled from the Iberian Peninsula, and Spain became the kingdom most **loyal** to Roman Catholicism. To maintain the **financial resources** of the new Spanish king-dom, explorers, such as Christopher Columbus, were sent to seek riches beyond the seas. It was also in 1492 that Columbus discovered the New World.

The Spanish flag is red and yellow. It symbolizes the red blood shed during the battle to destroy the Islamic nation and conquer the New World, and the yellow is the golden wealth gained from conquest. Due to the opposition between Christianity and Islam, Europe **ironically** gained much science and knowledge from the Islamic world. This **spurred** the Renaissance.

アーサー・C・クラーク氏です。というの
も、中世以前に地中海世界で長年培われた
文明の多くは、イスラム世界の中で**保存さ
れ、培養されて**いたからです。当時、バグ
ダッドの図書館には世界中の知識が書物と
して保管されていたと言われています。

アーサー・C・クラーク

　その後、ヨーロッパでも過去の文明を見
直そうと、ルネサンス運動がはじまります
が、それはトゥール・ポワティエ間の戦い
から700年も後のことでした。ルネサンス期のヨーロッ
パの知識人は、さまざまなことをイスラム社会から学ん
だのです。

　1096年から、ヨーロッパではイスラム社会に対して何
度も**十字軍**を派遣し、**聖地エルサレム**を奪還しようとし
ます。キリスト教社会とイスラム教社会との対立はここ
まで遡れるわけです。同時に、西ヨーロッパではイベリア
半島からイスラム教世界を駆逐し、キリスト教国を打ち
立てようという運動も起こります。そして、1492年にイ
ベリア半島からイスラム教徒が駆逐され、スペインはロ
ーマ・カトリックに最も**忠誠を誓った**王国となったので
す。この新生スペイン王国の**財源**を維持するため、コロ
ンブスなどの探検家が富を求めて海の彼方へと派遣され
ました。コロンブスが新大陸を発見したのも、同じ1492
年のことでした。

クリストファー・コロンブス

　スペインの国旗は赤と黄色によって彩られています。
それはイスラム教国を滅ぼし、新大陸を征服する戦いで
流された血の赤と、それによって得られた黄金の富を黄
色で象徴しているのです。しかし、実はキリスト教とイ
スラム教との戦いによって、ヨーロッパ世界は**皮肉にも**、
イスラム圏から多くの科学や知識を輸入したのでした。

People of Middle Eastern descent resent the fact that many in the world forget these events and simply dismiss Muslim culture as **barbaric** compared with the scientific culture of the West. This pride, together with the Palestinian issue, which has become increasingly confused with the subsequent emergence of Israel, stirs their hearts and minds.

In fact, throughout the long history of the Middle Ages, it was Muslim societies that were more **tolerant** of other religions. In Islamic societies, freedom of religion was guaranteed as long as taxes were paid. However, this fact is already considered a thing of the past, and the image of Islam as a stubborn religion that excludes other beliefs has taken root. This is despite the fact that both Islam and Christianity originally came from the same monotheistic **religion**.

In recent years, the turmoil in the Middle East has led to the emergence of **Islamic fundamentalists** who have engaged in radical terrorist activities, which has led to prejudice against Islam in the Christian community. However, we should not forget the fact that in the US, the FBI is more nervous about terrorist activities by **Christian extremists**.

It seems that it will take more time for monotheistic religions to learn to respect each other's differences and **coexist**. Until such an ideal is fulfilled, Middle Eastern immigrants to the US are likely to continue to feel frustrated by ignorance of their roots.

▶ monotheistic ➔ p.120

これがルネサンス運動にも**拍車をかけた**のです。

　中東系の人々は、世界の多くの人がこうした事実を忘れ、ただ欧米の文化が科学的で、イスラム世界は**野蛮である**と断じることに、憤りを覚えます。このプライドと、その後のイスラエルの登場で混迷を深めたパレスチナ問題とが、彼らの心をかき乱します。

　実は、中世の長い歴史の中で、他の宗教に**寛容**だったのはイスラム教社会の方でした。イスラム社会では税金さえ納めれば信仰の自由は保障されました。しかし、こうした事実もすでに過去のこととされ、イスラム教は他の宗教を排除する頑なな宗教というイメージが定着しているわけです。イスラム教もキリスト教も元は同じ**一神教**であるにもかかわらず、です。

　近年、中東での混乱が原因で**イスラム原理主義者**が現れ、過激なテロ活動を行ったことが、キリスト教社会でのイスラム教に対する偏見につながりました。ただ、忘れてはならないのは、アメリカでは、**キリスト教過激派**によるテロ活動にFBIがより神経を尖らせているという事実もあることです。

　一神教同士がお互いの違いを尊重し**共存する**には、まだまだ時間がかかりそうです。そんな理想が成就するまで、アメリカに移住する中東系移民たちは、自らのルーツへの無知に対して、苛立ちを抱き続けることになりそうです。

第3章

Key word

MONOTHEISTIC 一神教の

　字義どおり「唯一の神しかいないと信じる」ことを表し、「一神教」という名詞は monotheism といいます。本文にもあるように、イスラム教、キリスト教、ユダヤ教の3つは一神教の典型とされています。対義語は「複数の神を信じる（polytheistic）」、「多神教（polytheism）」です。日本は無宗教ともいわれますが、神社にお参りしたり結婚式を挙げたり、家に神棚を祀ったりするような神道の影響は今もなお私たちの生活に根差しており、「八百万の神」を信仰する多神教国家ともいえます。宗教や信仰に関する話題は非常にセンシティブですが、日本の宗教について少しでも英語で語れるようにしておくとよいでしょう。

例文

The three monotheistic religions with the most followers are Christianity, Judaism, and Islam.
一神教の中で最も信者が多いのは、キリスト教、ユダヤ教、イスラム教の3つだ。

The professor explained the establishment of ancient monotheism based on archeological evidence.
教授は古代の一神教の成立を考古学的な証拠に基づいて説明した。

Shinto is a polytheistic religion unique to Japan.
神道は日本に固有の多神教である。

 あなたはどう答える？

What is the history of faith in Japan?
日本にはどのような信仰の歴史がありますか？

ヒント ▶ 狩猟採集をしていた頃からの自然信仰や神道、6世紀に伝来した仏教、戦国時代に伝来したキリスト教、近現代に成立した新興宗教などありますが、国教は定められていません。

覚えておくと便利な単語、表現

- ☐ **established religion**　国教
- ☐ **grant freedom of worship**　信仰の自由を認める
- ☐ **have no religion**　無宗教である

第13話
宗教と科学の課題を突きつける
インドのコロナ禍

Article 13
India's Covid Disaster Puts Religion and Science on the Line

As Covid-19 devastates India, deaths go undercounted.
—— New York Times

（コロナがインド社会をむしばむ中、死者数の実態も予想よりさらに
ひどくなっている）

India celebrates the spring festival of Holi around the 20th of March every year. It is one of the three major festivals of Hinduism and is held to **pray for a good harvest** and expel demons. During the festival, people throw colored water at each other to ward off evil spirits. Children, in particular, tend to enjoy splashing colored water on passersby.

Hinduism is deeply rooted and faithfully practiced in India. If you visit the famous Hindu sanctuary of Varanasi (Banares), you will find a large number of devotees coming down from stairways called ghats to **bathe** in the Ganges River. They wash their bodies in the river water, rinse their mouths, and **recite prayers**. From there, walk through the riverside alleys for a while, and you will suddenly come to a square with countless piles of firewood. As you pass through an old building and emerge on the banks of the Ganges River, you'll find these pieces of firewood are used to cremate the dead.

Dogs and cows roam around the corpses as they are cremated in the "Sacred Fire." It is not easy to forget the scene of animals eating a corpse's flesh after it was burned.

To sum up, religious festivals are held on the Ganges River, the dead are burned, and people bathe in the water of the river nearby.

In April 2021, after the Holi festival in Varanasi and other parts of India, the coronavirus spread rapidly. With the conditions brought by the pandemic, **medical care collapsed** in many places, and instead of being brought to Varanasi for cremation, the dead were burned in city squares. Due to lack of medical supplies, infected family members were sometimes left with no

インドは毎年3月の20日前後にホーリー祭という春祭りを祝います。これはヒンドゥー教の三大祭りの一つで、**豊作祈願**や悪魔払いを目的として繰り広げられます。祭りでは、魔除けに起源を持つという色水をかけ合います。特に、子どもが道ゆく人にあたりかまわず色水をかけることで知られています。

インドはヒンドゥー教が深く浸透した国家です。ヒンドゥー教の聖地として有名なヴァラナーシ（ベナレス）を訪ねると、ガートという階段からガンジス川に下りて、**沐浴をしている**多数の信者がいます。身体中に川の水を浴び、口をすすぎ、**祈りを唱え**ます。そこから川沿いの路地をしばらく歩けば、いきなり無数の薪が積まれた広場に出ます。その脇から古い建物をくぐってガンジス川のほとりに出ると、川辺に薪が積まれ、死者が火葬されています。

ホーリー祭（イメージ）

第3章

何体もの遺体が「聖なる火」と呼ばれる火によって荼毘に付されるなか、犬と牛がその遺体の周りをうろうろとしています。遺体が焼かれたあと、その肉を食べている様子はなかなか忘れられるものではありません。

つまり、ガンジス川で宗教的な祭典が行われ、死者が焼かれ、その近くで人々がその川の水につかって沐浴をしているわけです。

そしてヴァラナーシをはじめ、インド各地でホーリー祭のあと、2021年4月になってコロナが急拡大したのです。各地で**医療崩壊**が起こり、ヴァラナーシに運ばれて荼毘に付されることもなく、人々は街の広場で火葬されました。医療機器の不足で、罹患者の家族が酸素ボンベを取り合い騒然となることもありました。

choice but to fight over oxygen cylinders.

Regardless of assistance from all over the world, vaccination procedures could not keep up, and frighteningly, the number of daily cases exceeded 350,000.

In response to the **infection situation** in India, the US has decided to **restrict entry** from India. It has temporarily banned people who are not US citizens from entering the country from India.

Over 4 million people of Indian descent live in the US, and restrictions on travel to and from their home country of India are a great stress for them. In fact, people of Indian descent in the US play a particularly active role in its society. Compared with the Japanese and other groups, Indians, with their **assertive** and self-promoting, communicative culture, are able to adapt well to American society, and their activities are diverse, ranging from education to medicine to the high-tech industry.

When one thinks of such Indian activities and traditional Indian people bathing in Varanasi, it makes one consider again the **complex structure** of Indian society and the psychology and culture of the Indian people, where religion and science coexist.

The World Health Organization (WHO) has been concerned about the impact of religious rituals on the spread of infection since the discovery of the **mutated coronavirus** in India. However, despite warnings about the spread of infection, especially to enthusiastic devotees during the Holi festival, countless believers still gathered at holy sites, huddled together, and immersed themselves in **religious rituals**. And many of these people were later found, some dead and some alive, on the streets as the infection spread rapidly.

► infection → p.128

　世界各地から支援の手が差し伸べられても、ワクチン接種も追いつかず、1日の感染者が35万人を上回るという恐ろしい毎日が続いたのです。

　インドの**感染状況**を受け、アメリカはインドからの**入国制限**に踏み切りました。アメリカ国籍を持っていない人のインドからの入国を一時的に禁止したのです。

　アメリカには400万人を超すインド系の人々が住んでいます。彼らにとって母国インドとの往来の制限は大きなストレスです。実際、アメリカのインド系の人々はあちこちで活躍しています。日本人などと比較して、**主張が強く**、自己アピールも旺盛なコミュニケーション文化を持つインド人は、アメリカ社会にうまく適応でき、その活動舞台は教育、医療、ハイテク産業に至るまで多様で、インド系のプログラマーや企業家、さらには科学者の多さに驚かされます。

　そんなインド人の活動とヴァラナーシで沐浴する伝統的なインド人の姿を思い浮かべると、改めてインド社会の**複雑な構造**、宗教と科学とが同居したインド人の心理や文化について考えさせられます。

　WHO（世界保健機関）は、インドで**コロナの変異ウイルス**が発見されたときから、宗教儀式が感染拡大に与える影響を懸念していました。しかし、特にホーリー祭で熱狂する信者に対する感染拡大への警告があったにもかかわらず、やはり無数の信者が聖地に集まり、体を寄せ合って**宗教儀式**に没頭しました。そしてそんな人々が、その後の急激な感染拡大の中で、路上で生死をさまよったのです。

Never before has such a contradictory coexistence of religion and science been witnessed.

India has sent out scientists and mathematicians to the world, and has greatly contributed to the development of advanced industries in the US. The US is strengthening exchanges and cooperation with India, partly because of its tense relationship with China. In order to check China's advance into the Indian Ocean and South China Sea, it has been focusing on diplomacy with India, which has been in conflict with China over the **territorial dispute** over Kashmir.

It is also worth noting that in India, whose international influence is increasing, there is a deep-rooted **far-right movement** called Hindu nationalism, which rejects Western civilization and claims that Hinduism is the supreme religion. Conflicts with neighboring Muslim Pakistan are also spurring such movements.

The issue of the coexistence of religion and science is an important topic facing many parts of the world. The two contradictory ways of thinking—respecting tradition and favoring science—coexist among individuals of all nations, and repeatedly come into conflict.

This issue is not limited to India, but is common to all religions, including Western Christian societies and Middle Eastern Muslim ones.

　宗教と科学とが、これほどまでに矛盾しながら同居している様子を見せつけられたことはありません。

　インドが、世界に科学者や数学者を輩出し、アメリカの先端産業の育成にも大きく貢献しています。アメリカは中国との緊張関係もあり、インドとの交流や連携を強化しています。インド洋と南シナ海への中国の進出を牽制する意味からも、元々カシミールの**領有権問題**などで中国との対立が続くインドとの外交には力を入れてきたのです。

　そんな国際的な影響力を増すインドの中に、ヒンドゥー・ナショナリズムという西欧文明を排斥し、ヒンドゥー教こそが最高の宗教であるとする**極右運動**が根強くあることも知っておきたい事実です。隣国のイスラム教国パキスタンとの対立もそうした運動に拍車をかけています。

　宗教と科学との共存という課題は、世界の多数の地域が抱えている重要なテーマです。伝統を重んじながらも、科学的であるべきという二つの矛盾した意識が、あらゆる国家の個々人の中に同居し、葛藤を繰り返しているのです。

　これはインドに限ったことではなく、欧米のキリスト教社会、中東のイスラム教社会など、あらゆる宗教世界に共通した課題なのです。

▶カシミールはインド北部とパキスタン北東部の国境付近にひろがる山岳地域。インド・パキスタン・中国の3か国がその領有権を主張しており、インドはパキスタンと3度、中国と1度戦争をしているが、所属は未定である。

第3章

Key word

INFECTION 感染（症）

　「病原体が人や動物の体内に定着すること」、その「感染によって引き起こされる病気」です。関連して、infectは「〔～に〕感染させる、うつす」という他動詞で、「感染する」というときはbe infectedと表します。形容詞infectiousは「〔病気が〕感染性の、感染力のある」という意味です。

　ちなみに、感染対策として対人距離を確保する「ソーシャル・ディスタンス」ですが、英語でsocial distanceというと本来は「異なる人種や民族、階級などの間に存在する社会的距離」を意味し、日本語に対応する英語はsocial distancingが多く用いられています。ただ、実際に社会的距離を置くわけではないため、物理的距離を意味するphysical distancingを使うことも増えているようです。

例 文

Those symptoms are due to infection.
その症状は感染によるものだ。

I was infected with the virus even though I washed my hands and gargled frequently.
手洗い、うがいを頻繁にしていても、そのウイルスに感染した。

Mumps is an infectious disease.
おたふく風邪は感染性のある病気（感染症）だ。

 あなたはどう答える？

Please tell us about the territorial issues that Japan is facing.
日本が抱えている領有権問題について教えてください。

> ヒント　政府が問題として表明しているのは、ロシアとの間にある北方四島と韓国との間にある竹島です。中国との間にある尖閣諸島に関しては未解決の問題は存在しないとしています。

覚えておくと便利な単語、表現

☐ **be in conflict with**　～と対立する
☐ **seek a peaceful solution to**　～の平和的解決を模索する
☐ **territorial dispute over**　～を巡る領有権問題

第14話
フランス大統領選挙の結果から見る EUの行方

Article 14
The Future of the European Union after the French Presidential Elections

"British voters delivered stunning blows to the country's two main political parties in European elections, underlining the growing polarization over the effort to leave the European Union but signaling no obvious way out of the Brexit deadlock."

—— Wall Street Journal

（イギリスの有権者は、二大政党がヨーロッパの選挙の中でEU離脱について対立が深まり、イギリス離脱の出口が見えなくなっていることに当惑のため息をついている）

The reelection of **incumbent** Emmanuel Macron in the 2022 French presidential election is a positive sign for the future of the EU. While the unity of the EU was being **brought into question** by Russia's invasion of Ukraine, the reelection of Hungarian prime minister

フランスの極右政党「国民連合（RN）」を率いるマリーヌ・ル・ペン

Viktor Orbán, who is close to Russian president Vladimir Putin, and the rise of Marine Le Pen, a right-wing presidential candidate who was originally **skeptical** of the EU, in France, had made the future of the election **uncertain**. Although it was a close race, the West is currently relieved that President Macron was reelected.

The process of the United Kingdom's exit from the European Union, known as Brexit, involved difficult negotiations between the United Kingdom and the European Union.

To begin with, the internal situation in the United Kingdom was also complicated. Northern Ireland has been part of the United Kingdom for many years. However, Ireland, located to its south, had in the past gained independence from the British colonies and joined the EU as a **sovereign nation**. If Brexit goes ahead, there will also be the issue of how to manage the border between Northern Ireland and Ireland. In addition, the will of the Scottish people is another challenge. Scotland has been **reluctant** about Brexit, and there has been strong momentum for independence there. If Brexit is forced through without the consent of Northern Ireland and Scotland, coordination with these regions will not be easy.

2022年のフランス大統領選挙で、**現職**のエマニュエル・マクロン氏が再選されたことは、EUの未来に明るい兆しとなりました。ウクライナへのロシアの侵攻でEUの結束が**問われ**ているなかで、ハンガリーではロシアのプーチン大統領と親密なオルバン・ヴィクトル首相が再選され、フランスでも元々 EU に**懐疑的**だった右派の大統領候補マリーヌ・ル・ペン氏が台頭したことで、選挙の行方が**不透明**になっていたのです。接戦であったとはいえ、結果としてマクロン大統領が再選されたことに西側諸国は安堵しているのが現状です。

Brexitと呼ばれたイギリスのEU離脱の過程では、イギリスとEUの交渉が難航しました。

そもそもイギリスの内情も複雑でした。イギリスは長年北アイルランドをイギリスの一部としています。しかし、その南に位置するアイルランドは、過去にイギリスの植民地から独立し、**主権国家**としてEUに加わっています。もし、Brexitが進めば、北アイルランドとアイルランドとの国境をどう管理するかという課題も出てきます。さらに、スコットランドの民意も課題の一つです。

131

So what about the EU side? Recently, there have been fears regarding the rise of right-wing parties that are skeptical of the EU in some of the major EU countries. One was France. Also, in the Netherlands, there was even a move by a right-wing party that is negative toward the EU to gain a majority in the **parliament**.

One of the EU's challenges is immigration. Although EU countries are suffering from **labor shortages** and **low growth**, the rapid increase in immigration is changing their national identities. Many people also argue that Germany and France, the dominant countries in the EU, are **being forced to pay for** the **economic disparity** with southern and eastern European countries that are suffering from economic difficulties in the enlarged EU.

From the EU's point of view, it does not want the move to leave the EU to spill over into the mainland. There is also the issue of how to deal with the 1.2 million British citizens already living in the EU and the estimated 3.2 million EU nationals living in the United Kingdom. Both areas are also home to many immigrants from the Middle East and Africa who have migrated to Europe. Many challenges remain as to how the UK will conclude **customs**, trade, and immigration agreements with the EU and how the EU will approve them in accordance with EU rules.

It will take a lot of work to resolve and sort these issues out.

For the time being, the UK is trying to move all existing agreements with the EU into UK **domestic law** and is taking time to make adjustments. Some experts believe it will take as

▶ immigrant ➔ p.138

スコットランドはBrexitに**消極的な**地域で、独立の機運
も旺盛でした。もし、北アイルランドとスコットランド
の同意なくしてBrexitを強行した場合、これらの地域と
の調整は容易ではありません。

　では、EU側はどうでしょう。最近、EUの主要国の中
で、EUに懐疑的な右派政党の台頭が危惧されていまし
た。その一つがフランスだったのです。また、オランダ
でも、EUに否定的な右派勢力が議会の過半を狙う動きも
あったほどです。

　EUの課題の一つが移民問題です。**労働者不足と低成長**
に悩むEU諸国ではあるものの、急速な移民の増加はそれ
ぞれの国のアイデンティティを変えようとしています。
また、EU内の持てる国であるドイツやフランスが、EU
が拡大した中で経済難に苦しむ南ヨーロッパや東欧諸国
との経済格差のつけを払わされていると主張する人々が
多いのも事実です。

　EUから見れば、EU脱退の動きが地域内に波及してほ
しくはありません。かつ、すでにEU内に居住する120万
人のイギリス人や、イギリス内に居住する320万人とも
言われるEU諸国の人々への扱いも課題となります。どち
ら側にも、ヨーロッパに移住してきた中東やアフリカか
らの**移民**も多く居住しています。イギリスがEUとの**関税**
や貿易・移民協定をどう締結し、それをEUがEUの規則
に沿って承認するにはどうするかという無数の課題が残
ります。

　これらを整理解決するには相当の手間が必要です。

　イギリスは、とりあえず現在あるEUとの協定をすべ
てイギリスの**国内法**に移行し、時間をかけて調整しよう
と試みています。その作業が完了し、イギリスが完全に

第3章

long as 10 years for this process to be completed and for the UK to entirely exit the EU.

However, under current EU regulations, when a nation announces its intention to leave, the **transition period** is two years. That was far too short a period for the UK. There are still many people in the UK who insist on returning to the EU. However, few parties are willing to hold another **referendum** and ask whether they want to remain in the EU at this stage.

In fact, after more than half a century of extremely strong cooperation among European nations, even if a nation were to leave at great financial and human expense, it cannot change the framework of the larger partnership that is Europe. Nevertheless, the possibility that the idea of Brexit will continue to affect France, Italy, the Netherlands, and Germany, and thus **damage** the very foundations of the EU itself, has not faded.

So will a **weakened** EU benefit Russia, China, and the US? It is not a simple question, as **economic upheaval** and social unrest in the EU itself have a great potential to **ignite** a crisis in global financial markets. Japan, the US, and even China have already invested heavily in the region. And now that Russia has invaded Ukraine, the EU itself must seem even more valuable.

Despite the **uncertainty** of immigration and people's **adherence** to their own culture and traditions, the number of refugees and immigrants continues to increase as they escape chaos in the Middle East and North Africa. It is true that the large increase in the proportion of foreign immigrants in London's population has given Britain a sense of crisis.

EU圏の外に出るには10年は必要という専門家もいるのです。

　しかし、現在のEUの規定では、国家がEU離脱を表明した場合、その**移行期間**は2年とされています。それはあまりにも短い期間でした。イギリス国内には、依然としてEU復帰を主張する人が多くいます。しかし、今の段階で再び**国民投票**を行いEUへの残留を問いかけようとする政党はほとんどないのです。

　実際のところ、ヨーロッパ諸国が極めて強く連携して半世紀以上の年月が経過した現在、たとえ国家が多大の税金と人的費用を投じて離脱をしても、ヨーロッパという大きな連携の枠を変えることはできないはずです。とはいえ、Brexitの発想がこれからもフランスやイタリア、さらにオランダやドイツに影響を与え、EUそのものの根幹に**打撃を与える**可能性が消え去ったわけではないのです。

　では、EUが**弱体化**すれば、ロシアや中国、そしてアメリカを利することになるのでしょうか。そんな単純なものではありません。EUそのものでの**経済の乱高下**や社会不安は、そのまま世界の金融市場に**飛び火する**可能性が大きくあります。日本もアメリカも、さらに中国もすでに多額の投資をこの地域に行っているのです。ましてロシアがウクライナに侵攻した現在、EUそのものの存在価値は大きくなっているはずです。

　移民の流入への**不安**、自国の文化や伝統への**固執**というセンチメンタリズムをよそに、中東や北アフリカでの混乱に押されて、難民や移民は増え続けます。ロンドンの人口に占める海外からの移住者の比率の大幅な増加がイギリスに危機感を与えたことは事実でしょう。似た状況はヨーロッパ各地に見られます。

第3章

Similar situations can be found throughout Europe. With every election that occurs in the EU's major countries, people continue to question the future of the ever-changing European Union.

　これからも EU の主要国での選挙のたびに、人々は EU
の今後がどうなるのか戦々恐々とするのではないでしょ
うか。

Key word

IMMIGRANT 〔外国からの〕移民

　「外国から定住や仕事のために移住してくる人」を指します。同じ「移民」を表す名詞でも、emigrant は反対に「外国へ定住や仕事のために移住していく人」、migrant は「よりよい仕事や生活を求めて場所を移る人」という意味です。migrant には「季節労働者、渡り鳥」の意味もあるのでイメージしやすいかもしれません。

　ちなみに同じ「外国から移住してくる人」でも、「難民」である refugee は「亡命者」という訳もあるように、紛争や迫害によって命の危険があるためにやむを得ず逃げてきたというニュアンスが含まれます。

....

例文

America is a land of immigrants.
アメリカは移民の国だ。

The ship carried hundreds of emigrants to the new continent.
その船は何百人もの移民を乗せて新大陸に向かった。

Japan has not opened its doors to refugees.
日本は難民に対する門戸が開かれていない。

？ あなたはどう答える？

What kind of cooperation does Japan have with foreign countries?
日本は海外の国々とどのような協力関係を結んでいますか？

ヒント　国際連合をはじめ主要国として G7 や G20 に参加しており、またアジアの一員として APEC や ASEAN+3、RCEP や TPP などにも加盟し、地域の経済協力に貢献しています。

覚えておくと便利な単語、表現

☐ **engage in economic cooperation**　経済協力を行う
☐ **join**　加盟する
☐ **leading nations of the world**　世界の主要国

138

第15話
女王の死去から見えてくる
イギリス王室の1000年のレガシー

Article 15
The Queen's Death Reveals the Thousand-Year Legacy of the British Royal Family

The long reign of Queen Elizabeth II was marked by her strong sense of duty.

—— BBC

（クイーンエリザベス2世の長い治世は、彼女の強い〔王としての〕義務によって支えられていた）

The death of Queen Elizabeth was widely reported around the world. After World War II, Queen Elizabeth **ascended the throne** at a time when British colonies were becoming independent, and her country's national influence was declining to a level far beyond what it had been in the 19th century.

However, it can be said that she was a virtuous ruler who splendidly restored Britain's lost authority through cooperation with the world. Behind her actions as queen was a system unique to England. It is a culture and system that England has developed over a period of a thousand years, which is different from the **Japanese imperial family**.

"Common" is a word that you should know in relation to the **British royal family**. Originally, it comes from the Latin word for "to be shared generally."

The **monarch** of England depends on "the support of the common people."

Since the 13th century, England has evolved its national system through many feuds between the royal family and the nobility, or between landlords and citizens. In the olden days, kings strengthened their power base and aimed for absolute authority in administration, the **judiciary**, and even diplomacy, which was called **royal prerogative**. However, in medieval Europe, the powers of the Pope, the King, and even the Holy Roman Empire were intermingled, each fighting for supremacy. The first to resist the English king's attempts to increase his own power were the nobles and other influential people who were **exhausted** by the war.

In 1215, they revolted against King John of England and forced him to recognize their claim that even kings should rule

► common → p.148

エリザベス女王の死去は、世界中で大きく報道されました。戦後、イギリスの植民地が各地で独立し、国家としての影響力が19世紀とは比較にならないほど凋落したときに、エリザベス女王は王位に就きました。

エリザベス2世

しかし、彼女はイギリスが失いつつあった権威を、むしろ世界との協調の中で見事に回復させた名君といえそうです。そうした彼女の王としての行動を支える背景にはイギリス独特の制度がありました。それは日本の皇室のあり方とは一味異なる、まさにイギリスが1000年という年月をかけて作り上げてきた文化であり制度なのです。

"Common"という言葉を知っておくとイギリス王室のことがよくわかります。元々ラテン語の「一般に共有されること」という言葉がその語源です。

イギリスの王は文字通り、「イギリス国民の共有」の上に成り立っているのです。

イギリスは13世紀以来、何度も王室と貴族、あるいは地主や市民との確執を経て国の制度を進化させ、現在に至っています。その昔、王は自らの権力基盤を強化し、王の大権と呼ばれる行政や司法、さらには外交での専制を目指していました。しかし、中世のヨーロッパは教皇と国王、さらには神聖ローマ帝国などの権力が入り乱れ、それぞれが覇権を求めて争っていました。そこに参戦して自らの権力を高めようとしたイギリス王に最初に抵抗したのが、戦争により疲弊した貴族などの有力者でした。

イングランド王ジョン
（失地王）

1215年に彼らは当時のイギリス王ジョンに対して立ち上がり、王であっても法に従って国を統治するべきだ

第3章

the country according to the law. The result was the Magna Carta.

The Magna Carta is still incorporated into the **British Constitution**. "Common Law" is a term often used by the English when talking about law, meaning a body of law that has been handed down by the people. Since the Magna Carta, the subsequent Puritan Revolution, and the "Bill of Rights" of the Glorious Revolution, the common law has been the law that has been passed down through the process of limiting the power of the king and establishing **parliamentary democracy**, following the customary relationship between the king, the powerful, the people, and Parliament. The British Constitution is an accumulation of institutions, **oaths**, and declarations established over time. This is what makes the British system of political legislation quite different from the constitutions of many other countries, such as the constitution of Japan.

Thus, surprisingly, the king or queen can **theoretically** still exercise great powers in England. In other words, the monarch's power to dissolve parliament and to make decisions in diplomatic negotiations has remained unrestricted. The **Cabinet** and the Parliament are supposed to make the final decisions on administration, diplomacy, and legislation, and this custom of "reigns but does not rule" has been passed down to the present day.

Therefore, compared to the Japanese imperial family, the British royal family is more **outspoken** about politics. In the case of the Japanese imperial family, while the emperor's involvement in past wars was pointed out, any intentional political statements were considered taboo, and from the postwar Showa Emperor to the present, successive emperors and members of

という主張を認めさせます。そうして交付されたのがマグナ・カルタでした。

マグナ・カルタは**イギリスの憲法**の中に今でも組み込まれています。イギリス人が法律を語るときよく使う言葉に、「コモン・ロー」があります。一般的には慣習法と訳されますが、つまり人々によって受け継がれた法体系のことを意味します。マグナ・カルタ以来、その後の清教徒革命、さらには名誉革命での「権利の章典」を経て王の権限を制限し、**議会制民主主義**を確立してゆく過程で、王と有力者や民衆、さらには議会との関係を慣例として踏襲し、法制化してきたものがコモン・ローです。イギリスの憲法はその時々に定められた制度や**誓約書**、宣言書が蓄積された集合体なのです。それが、日本国憲法など多くの国の憲法とはまったく異なるイギリスの政治立法制度の特徴といえます。

したがって驚くことに、イギリスでは**理論上**、国王は今でも大権を行使することはできるのです。つまり議会を解散したり、外交交渉での決裁をしたりという様々な大権は、具体的には制限されないまま現在に至っています。それを今までの慣習によって抑制し、そうした行政や外交、立法上の最終決裁を**内閣**や議会が行うことになっているわけで、「君臨すれども統治せず」という慣習として現在に受け継がれているのです。

ですから、日本の皇室と比較して、イギリスの王室は政治に対してもより**踏み込んだ発言**をします。日本の皇室の場合は、天皇と過去の戦争への関与が指摘されるなか、意図的な政治的発言は一切タブーとされ、戦後の昭和天皇から現在まで、歴代の天皇や皇族が公の場所で国の政策や外交に対して発言をすることはありません。

第3章

the imperial family have never spoken publicly about national policy or diplomacy.

In comparison, the British royal family is relatively open. When Queen Elizabeth II ascended to the throne, she made a speech in which she stated that the future of the UK should not be about reigning over colonial territories, but rather about cooperation with Europe and other countries. It is also well known that the new King Charles, who succeeded to the throne, frequently included **concerns** about environmental issues in his speeches in the past.

This can be seen as a **remnant** of the fact that the king or queen has great power, although it cannot be exercised in reality. At the same time, there is an invisible tension and respect between the people and the royal family. The late Queen Elizabeth II was always aware of the public's judgment of the royal family. The tension between the people and the royal family **came to the surface** when Princess Diana died in a car accident and the people were disappointed that the royal family acted so coldly afterwards. Later, both Queen Elizabeth II and Prince Charles worked hard to rebuild the authority of the royal family by getting closer to the people and actively interacting with them abroad.

In other words, the king or queen really is the monarch of England. Although there are various opinions about the **monarchy** among the people, as long as the royal family remains popular and familiar to the public, the king or queen will continue to function as the spiritual pillar of the English people. On the occasion of the death of Queen Elizabeth II, broadcasters, such as the BBC, continued to report the news in **mourning clothes**, while the Prime Minister and former Prime Ministers paid their respects on the occasion of the succession of the new King

それと比較するとイギリスの王室はオープンです。エリザベス2世が即位したときも、今後のイギリスのあり方は植民地上に君臨するのではなく、ヨーロッパをはじめとした諸国との協調を大切にするべきだというスピーチをしています。また、王位を継承したチャールズ新国王が、過去には環境問題への**懸念**を頻繁にスピーチなどで盛り込んでいたことは有名な話です。

これは、現実的には行使はできないものの、国王に大権があることの**名残**ともいえます。そこには国民と王室との見えない緊張関係と敬意とが同時に存在しています。亡くなったエリザベス2世は、常に国民の王室への評価を意識していました。特に、ダイアナ元妃が交通事故で亡くなり、王室があまりにもその死に対して冷たかったことに国民が失望したときなどは、まさに国民と王室との緊張が**表面化しました**。その後、エリザベス2世もチャールズ皇太子も、より一層国民に接近し、海外との交流も積極的に行うことで、王室の権威を再構築することに懸命だったのです。

ダイアナ元妃

つまり、イギリスでは王は本当に王なのです。国民の中には**王制**に対して様々な意見はあるものの、王族が国民に親しまれ人気を維持している限り、王はイギリス人の精神的支柱として機能し続けることになります。今回エリザベス2世の死去にあたり、BBCなどの放送局のキャスターは**喪服**で報道を続け、首相や首相経験者が厳粛な姿でチャールズ新国王の王位継承やその儀式に敬意を払っているのも、イギリスでの民主主義を王室が積極的に支持してきたことによって、政治と王室との関係と伝

第3章

Charles to the throne and its ceremonies in a solemn manner, symbolizing that the relationship and tradition between politics and the royal family have been maintained through the royal family's active support for democracy in the UK.

The UK is divided into England and Scotland, and Wales and Northern Ireland, each of which is a distinct region, and has on several occasions been threatened with division for religious or political reasons. It is also important to note that the king of England is the king of each of these regions. Elizabeth II was the symbol that united them. There are also former British colonies around the world that still have the king as their **head of state**, such as Canada and Australia, which mourned the queen's death **on their behalf**. The queen's death and the subsequent **media coverage** brought into sharp relief these characteristics of the British nation that are difficult for Japanese to understand.

In a sense, all the experiences and accumulations since William of Normandy arrived in England from France in 1066 and established a new royal family there are directly reflected in the laws and customs of England today, and the repeated **trials and errors** in the form of the royal authority are directly reflected in the English tradition and the pride of the English people.

As a symbol of this pride, the months leading up to the news of the queen's death, her succession to the throne, and her funeral literally showed us a true face of England that we have not been able to see until now.

統が維持されてきたことを象徴的に表している現象といえましょう。

　イギリスはイングランドとスコットランド、そしてウェールズと北アイルランドという、それぞれ異なる地域に分かれ、時には宗教上、政治上の理由で分断される危機も何度かありました。イギリス王はそうした各地域の王であるという事実も知っておかなければなりません。エリザベス2世はこれらの異なる地域を統合する象徴でした。また、今でも世界中にイギリス王を**元首**と規定しているイギリスの元植民地もあり、カナダやオーストラリアなどがその**代表として**女王の死に対して喪に服しました。こうした日本人にはわかりにくいイギリスという国の特徴が、今回の女王の死去とその後の**報道**によって浮き彫りにされました。

　ある意味で、1066年にノルマンディー公ウィリアムがフランスからイギリスに上陸し、イギリスに新たな王室を樹立して以来、現在までのすべての経験と蓄積が、そのまま今のイギリスの法律や慣習に生きていて、そこで幾度も繰り返された王権のあり方への**試行錯誤**が、そのままイギリスの伝統として、イギリス人のプライドにもなっているわけです。

　そのプライドを象徴するように、今回の訃報から王位継承、女王の葬儀に至るひと月は、今まで我々が見ることのできなかったイギリスの素顔を文字通り見せてくれたのです。

第3章

Key word

COMMON 一般的な、公の

　イギリス社会ではこのcommonという言葉が広く使われています。例えば"the Commons [House of Commons]"といえば、イギリス議会の下院（庶民院）を表します。かつて国王と貴族が中心であった議会にcommmons（庶民階級）が招集されるようになり、現在では上院（貴族院）に優越し事実上の立法権限は庶民院にあります。また、イギリスには現在も"common"とつく地名がありますが、これは元々中世イングランドで地域経済の一部を構成していた、近隣住民による放牧・農業や生活のための「共有地」に由来します。日本語で「入会（地）」と訳されるcommonsは社会で「共有する」財産なのです。

例文

After serving in the House of Commons for a few years, she was appointed Secretary of State for Education.
彼女は数年間下院議員を務めた後、教育大臣に任命された。

Common lands are set aside for use by all members of a community.
共有地は共同体のすべてのメンバーが使用できるよう確保されている。

English has now become the common language of many nations in the world.
英語は今や世界の多くの国の共通言語になっている。

 あなたはどう答える？

What are the characteristics of the Imperial House of Japan?
日本の皇室にはどのような特徴がありますか？

> **ヒント**　皇族は日本国籍をもつ国民ですが、戸籍および名字をもちません。天皇とその男系血脈で構成され、皇室に嫁ぐのに国籍は問われません。天皇は国政に関与しない国の象徴です。

覚えておくと便利な単語、表現

☐ **not have any power over national politics**　国政に関する権能をもたない
☐ **patrilineal imperial succession**　男系の皇位継承
☐ **possess Japanese citizenship**　日本国籍を有する

第16話
極東情勢を左右する
日韓の対立の長い歴史

Article 16
The Long History of Conflict between Japan and South Korea and Its Effects on the Far East

Former Prosecutor General Yoon Seok-youl announced Tuesday that he will compete in the next presidential election in a bid to stop the "corrupt and incompetent" Moon Jae-in administration from extending its rule.

—— Korea Times

（前検察総長のユン・ソンニョル氏が、火曜日に次期大統領選挙への立候補を表明し、「汚職にまみれ、無能な」ムン・ジェイン政権の継承を阻止すると発表）

The South Korean presidential election held in the spring of 2022 **saw the appointment** of Yoon Suk-yeol, leader of the People's Power Party. Unlike the previous Moon Jae-in administration, the South Korean government is expected to improve its relations with Japan.

The **deterioration** of ties between Japan and South Korea is a challenge for the Far East. In addition to a lack of mutual understanding, there seems to be political exploitation of the conflict between the two countries.

Anti-Japanese sentiment in Korea is rooted in the fact that Korea was a Japanese colony for 35 years until the end of World War II. We should note, however, that the dislike for Japan goes even farther back than Korean independence.

When Japan was defeated in World War II, independence negotiations were held between Lyuh Woon-hyung, one of the leaders of the independence movement, and the Japanese governor-general who ruled Korea at the time. As a result, the People's Republic of Korea was established.

At that point, however, the Soviet Union had already **marched** into Pyongyang. The US also moved into Seoul after Japan's surrender, and each brought in its own rule of the peninsula, influenced by the postwar Cold War situation. Before Japan's defeat, the US, the UK, and the Soviet Union had agreed that Korea would be **placed under their trusteeship**.

▶ colony ➜ p.158

　韓国で2022年春に行われた大統領選挙では、「国民の力」を率いるユン・ソンニョル（尹錫悦）氏が**当選しました**。それまでのムン・ジェイン（文在寅）政権とは異なり、日本との関係の改善も期待されています。

　日韓関係の**悪化**は極東の課題です。そこにはお互いへの理解の欠如に加え、両国の対立を政治的に利用する動きも影響しているようです。

　韓国の**反日感情**は、第二次世界大戦が終わるまで35年間、韓国が日本の**植民地**だったことに起因しています。しかし、韓国の独立後にも、反日感情が醸成された背景があることにも注目すべきです。
　日本の敗戦時に、独立運動の指導者の一人ヨ・ウニョン（呂運亨）と当時韓国を支配していた日本の朝鮮総督府との間で独立のための話し合いが行われ、その結果、韓国には朝鮮人民共和国が成立したのです。

　しかし、その時点ですでにソ連はピョンヤンに**進軍し**ていました。さらに、日本の降伏を受けてアメリカもソウルに進駐し、それぞれが独自に半島の統治を始め、戦後の冷戦構造を持ち込んだのです。日本の敗戦以前にアメリカ、イギリス、ソ連の三国によって、韓国は**信託統治下に置かれる**ことが合意されていたのです。

ヤルタ会談に臨む（前列左から）チャーチル、ルーズベルト、スターリン。1945年2月4日から11日にかけて行われたこの会談では、朝鮮半島など日本の領土の処遇も秘密裏に決定された。

Therefore, the independence of Korea did not take into account the will of the people, partly due to the ignorance of the great powers about South Korea, and it was eventually **divided** into North Korea, which is a communist country, and South Korea, which is supported by the US and others. Due to this division, the Korean War **broke out** in 1950, claiming more than 5 million lives. One-sixth of the population of the Korean Peninsula was killed. Ironically, it was the **demand** for US forces during the Korean War that helped Japan recover from the devastation of the postwar period and paved the way for its **economic growth.**

Some South Koreans advocated the "Colonial Modernization Theory," which states that the country's modernization began during Japan's colonial period. A number of them happened to have backgrounds in military service in Japan during the colonial period or were involved in the Japanese rule. They became the source of the later **conservative forces** in Korea.

In contrast, those who advocated colonial dispossession became the source of the anti-establishment movement as progressives. They were also critical of Korea's role in the Cold War. In an attempt to advance a **democratic movement** with a Korean identity, they served as the driving force behind the overthrow of the pro-US, conservative Syngman Rhee administration.

However, in response to this move, conservatives executed a coup and established a military government. The central figure was Park Geun-hye's father, Park Chung-hee, a colonial-era military officer who had graduated from a Japanese military academy. Under his regime, the democratic movement was severely suppressed and relations with the US and Japan were strengthened. However, the democratic movement reemerged in response to

　そのため韓国の独立は列強の韓国に対する無知もあって、民意とは別のところで討議され、最終的には共産主義国である北朝鮮と、アメリカなどに支援された韓国とに**分断された**のです。その延長で1950年に**勃発した**朝鮮戦争では、500万を超える人命が奪われます。当時の朝鮮半島の人口の6人に1人が犠牲になったのです。皮肉なことに、日本は朝鮮戦争でのアメリカ軍の**需要**によって、戦後の荒廃から立ち直り、**経済成長**への道筋をつけたのです。

　韓国には日本の植民地時代に近代化が始まったとする「植民地近代化論」を唱える人がいました。彼らの中には植民地時代に日本で軍歴を持ったり、統治に関わったりした人たちもいて、のちの韓国の**保守勢力**の源流となったのです。

　それに対して、「植民地収奪論」を唱える人々は、進歩派として反体制運動の源流となりました。彼らは冷戦に韓国が翻弄されたことにも批判的でした。そして、韓国のアイデンティティをもって**民主化運動**を進めようとして、アメリカ寄りで保守系のイ・スンマン（李承晩）政権を倒す原動力となったのです。

　ところが、この動きに保守派がクーデターを起こし軍事政権を打ち立てます。その中心人物が、パク・クネ（朴槿恵）元大統領の父親で、植民地時代に日本の士官学校を卒業した経歴を持つ軍人であるパク・チョンヒ（朴正熙）でした。彼の政権下で、民主化運動は厳しく弾圧され、アメリカや日本との関係が強化されました。しかし、こうした**強権政治**に対して民主化運動が再燃します。

パク・チョンヒ（朴正熙）

第3章

153

these **authoritarian regimes.**

Then, President Park Chung-hee was assassinated due to a division within his administration. During the administration of his successor, Chun Do-hwan, the democratic movement developed into a **nationwide rebellion.** As seen in the Gwangju Uprising, much blood was spilled. The generation at the center of the democratization movement at that time was the generation born in the 1960s, who were university students in the 1980s. Since they were in their thirties in the 1990s when Korea became democratic, they were called the "386 Generation" (people born in the 1960s who joined the democratic movement in the 1980s and were in their thirties in the 1990s) in Korea. It was through them that Korea was reborn as a democratic nation.

This generation has a connection to the roots of those who originally advocated the theory of post-independence colonial dispossession. The generation of the democratization movement rejected previous compromises and also sought to reevaluate Japan's colonial period. This led to the rejection of past agreements between Japan and South Korea and **denunciations** of the comfort women and conscription issues.

Now that the 386 generation are in their 50s, new criticisms of the situation are shaking the political world as they continue to **benefit** from the political system they created. Commentaries have arisen that the ladder of democratization has not been passed on to the younger generations. Through such movements, activities calling for fairer and more just politics, **better rights for women**, etc. have sprouted. Some members of the new generation are critical of Japan-Korea relations that have become rigid due to the 386 generation, and they are becoming more aware of China's hard-line diplomacy toward South Korea.

　パク・チョンヒ大統領は政権内部の分裂により暗殺さ
れ、その後を継いだチョン・ドゥファン（全斗煥）政権時
に、民主化運動は**全国的な騒乱**へと発展したのです。1980
年5月に起きた光州事件に代表されるように、たくさんの
血も流されました。当時の民主化運動の中心となった世
代は1960年代に生まれ、80年代に大学生であった世代で
す。民主化された90年代には30代であったため、韓国で
は彼らのことを「386世代」（90年代に30代で80年代の
民主化運動に加わった60年代生まれの人々）と呼んでい
ました。彼らによって韓国は民主主義国家として再生さ
れたのです。

　この世代が、元々独立後の植民地収奪論を唱えた人々
のルーツにつながるのです。民主化運動の世代は以前の
妥協を否定し、日本の植民地時代への評価も見直そうと
しました。これが日韓での過去の合意を否定し、慰安婦
問題や徴用工問題などへの**糾弾**につながったのです。

　今では、そんな386世代が50代になり、彼ら自身が作
り上げた政治体制の中でその**恩恵を受けている**ことへの
新たな批判が、政界を揺るがしています。民主化のはしご
を若い世代に継承していない、という批判が起きている
のです。そうした動きを通して、より公平で公正な政治、
女性の権利向上などを求める活動が萌芽しました。彼ら
新世代は、386世代によって硬直した日韓関係に批判的な
人々もいて、むしろ韓国に強硬な外交を展開する中国へ
の警戒感の方が強まりつつあります。

第3章

Article 16

Thus, Korean politics has been struggling to **break free** from Japanese colonization and the turmoil that followed, with public opinion continuing to swing like a pendulum even now.

It is therefore essential for Japan to keep its antennae up to monitor the rapidly changing public opinion in South Korea. Strengthening personal ties with the new generation there and building a renewed Japan-South Korea relationship through cooperation is also important for the balance of international politics in the Far East.

　このように、韓国の政治は日本の植民地化からの**脱皮**とその後の混乱にもがきながら、世論が振り子のように揺れながら、現在に至っているのです。

　であれば日本は、激しく変化する韓国の世論へのアンテナをしっかりと立ててゆくことが肝要です。韓国での新しい世代との人的パイプを強化し、連携することによって新たな日韓関係を築くことは、極東での国際政治のバランスを考える上でも大切なことなのです。

ソウル南山公園にあるNソウルタワー

第3章

157

Key word

COLONY　植民地

　「本国からの移住者によって経済的に開発されその国の領土として従属する、主権をもたない地域」のことです。15世紀半ばの大航海時代から第二次世界大戦が勃発した20世紀前半にかけて、列強と呼ばれる大国は植民地を次々と獲得して覇権を争っていました。1960年12月14日の国連総会で採択された「植民地独立付与宣言」を契機に多くの植民地は主権を獲得しましたが、現在も独立を宣言しても国家承認されていない、またあえて主権ではなく内政自治権を獲得して独自外交をしている地域もあります。旧植民地では独立の前後に政情の不安定さから戦争や紛争によって血が流されたことも多く、私たちはその負の歴史を知っておくべきでしょう。

例文

Korea was a Japanese colony for about 35 years, from 1910 to 1945.
朝鮮は1910年から1945年までの約35年間、日本の植民地であった。

The colony declared independence and became a republic.
その植民地は独立を宣言し、共和国となった。

The 13 British colonies formed the original states of the United States.
13のイギリス植民地が合衆国の最初の州を形成した。

? あなたはどう答える？

How is the deterioration of Japan-Korea relations perceived in Japan?
日韓関係の悪化について日本ではどのように受け止めれられていますか？

ヒント　韓流文化の流行に伴い、韓国語の学習者や留学生の数が若者を中心に増えています。2022年夏の日韓の民間世論調査では双方の印象に改善傾向が見られています。

覚えておくと便利な単語、表現

☐ build a relationship through cooperation　協力して関係を築く
☐ indicate a trend toward improvement in　〜の改善傾向を示す
☐ public opinion survey　世論調査

第 4 章

世界経済の未来

Chapter 4

The Future of the Global Economy

第 17 話
世界経済の覇者を決める電気自動車

Article 17
Electric Vehicles Decide Who Will Dominate the World Economy

Germany plans to phase out the sale of combustion-engine vehicles to help meet its ambitious goal of getting 15 million electric vehicles on the road by 2030.

—— INSIDER

（ドイツは液体燃料車に替わる電気自動車の製作に対し、2030年までに1,500万台の電気自動車を走らせるよう支援するという野心的な目標を発表）

The German government, which just had **general elections** in 2021, has announced strong support for bringing 15 million electric vehicles into the world by 2030. The most important task of the new government, led by **center-left forces**, is to address environmental issues. In this context, the shift away from conventional engine cars that rely on liquid fuels is to be accelerated. Moreover, this seems to be part of a strategy to regain the market share of German cars in the US and other markets, and to overcome the **fierce competition** with rival Japanese cars, whose makers have been on the defensive. Of course, this move should affect the entire EU **auto industry**.

Meanwhile, Tesla, the American electric car pioneer, announced that it would invest 137 billion Japanese yen in its Shanghai plant to strengthen its **production capabilities**.

In Japan, there have been several announcements recently by Toyota, Nissan, and Honda about their next-generation vehicles.

However, one cannot simply assume that the widespread use of electric vehicles equals a solution to environmental problems. There are still questions about whether the **carbon dioxide emissions** from power generation, the manufacture of electric vehicle parts, and infrastructure development are lower than those from **conventional** hybrid vehicles, for example. Can **global warming** really be prevented without a change in power generation know-how? In this light, there is a strong suspicion that the move toward electrification is being driven by a political struggle for **hegemony** over who will hold industrial power in the next generation. Nevertheless, the outcome of this struggle for supremacy may become apparent in less than a decade.

► hegemony → p.168

2021年に**総選挙**が終わったばかりのドイツ政府が、2030年までに1500万台の電気自動車を世の中に送り出すために強い支援をすることを発表しました。**中道左派勢力**が主力となった新政権の最も重要な課題が、環境問題への取り組みです。その中で、従来の液体燃料に頼ったエンジン車からの脱却が加速されることになりました。しかも、これはアメリカなどでドイツ車のシェアを奪還し、どちらかというと守勢に立たされ続けていたライバルの日本車との**熾烈な競争**を克服する戦略の一環でもあるようです。もちろん、この動きはEUの**自動車業界**全体に影響を与えるはずです。

▶2022年の1年間にアメリカで販売された自動車のメーカー別ランキングは、1位GM（ゼネラルモーターズ）、2位トヨタ、3位フォードだった。（出典：MarkLines）

一方、アメリカの電気自動車のパイオニアであるテスラは、上海の工場に1370億円の投資を行い、**生産力**を強化すると発表しました。

当然日本でも、トヨタや日産、そしてホンダなどで、次世代に対応した車についての発表が何件か続いています。

しかし、電気自動車の普及イコール環境問題の解決と短絡的に考えることはできません。発電や電動車の部品製作、インフラ整備による**二酸化炭素の排出**が、従来のハイブリッド車等による排出量より少なくなるのか、疑問が残ります。発電のノウハウ自体の変革なしに、本当に**温暖化**は防げるのでしょうか。こう考えると、電動化への動きは、次世代の産業力をどこが握るかという**覇権**をめぐる政治的な背景に押されているのではないかという疑いも濃くなります。しかも、この覇権争いの結果は、今後10年に満たない間に顕在化するかもしれないのです。

第4章

When we are living in our own era, we tend to be **insensitive** to the changes occurring around us. However, when you meet a friend from your college days for the first time in several decades, for example, you can feel the **passage of time** from the changes in that person's appearance. If there is no such trigger, though, the passage of time can be difficult to detect.

It took less than 30 years for people's **mode of transportation** to change dramatically from horse-drawn carriages to automobiles. This transformed the cityscape and brought about major changes in industry, people's lives, and their occupations. It coincided with America's overtaking of Great Britain and its subsequent dominance in the industrial world. Horse-drawn carriages have helped people get around for thousands of years. Gasoline-powered vehicles have changed human lifestyles in the last 120 years. And in just the next decade, we may say goodbye to the **internal combustion engine**, which has been a part of our lives since the Industrial Revolution, and hello to the electric car, which will become our primary means of transportation.

We can see that technological innovation is **accelerating** rapidly along a sharp curve. Naturally, people's lifestyles will change along this curve as well. It is no exaggeration to say that the current coronavirus pandemic has been further stimulating such changes.

In fact, when the gasoline engine developed in the US and began to bring about changes in people's lifestyles, two incidents occurred. The first was the Spanish flu, which shook the world for two years from 1918. Thanks to innovations in transportation, the infection spread rapidly around the world, and the number of deaths reached tens of millions.

Then came the Great Depression of 1929. Just as the world

　我々は自らが生きている時代の中にいるときは、自身の周辺で起きている変化に**鈍感**になりがちです。しかし、例えば大学時代の友人に数十年ぶりに会ったとき、その人の面影の変化から**時の流れ**を実感するように、そうした年月が世の中に与えるインパクトがいかに甚大かは、何かのきっかけがなければ、なかなか察知できません。

　馬車から自動車へと人々の**移動手段**が大きく変化したのは、ほんの30年間に満たないできごとでした。それは、街の風景を一新させ、産業や人々の生活、職業に大きな変化をもたらしました。それは、ちょうどアメリカがイギリスを追い抜いて、それ以降の産業界で覇権を握る時期に一致します。馬車は数千年にわたって人々の移動を助けてきました。ガソリン車は直近の120年間に人類のライフスタイルを変化させました。そして、これからほんの10年先には、産業革命から人々の生活に深く関わってきた**内燃機関**に別れを告げ、電気自動車が移動の主要手段になろうとしているのです。

第4章

　技術革新が急激なカーブを描いて**加速**していることがよくわかります。当然、このカーブに沿う形で人々のライフスタイルも変化するはずです。そんなライフスタイルの変化に、さらに刺激を与えているのが、現在のコロナパンデミックであるといっても過言ではありません。

　実は、アメリカを核に開発されたガソリンエンジンが人々のライフスタイルに変化をもたらし始めたころ、2つの事件が起こっています。まずは、1918年から2年にわたって世界を震撼させたスペインかぜです。人々の移動手段の革新によって、感染はあっという間に世界に拡大し、死者数は数千万人に及びました。

　そして、次に起こったのが1929年の世界恐慌です。世

economy was beginning to link up, it also quickly spread from the United States to the rest of the world. And that panic contributed to the **rise of fascist governments**. After World War II, America became the most powerful nation in the world.

The world today must be wary of three things: pandemics and the resulting economic instability, and the growing race to develop the next generation of automobiles.

The steeper the innovation curve, the faster and more severe the impact of pandemics and stock market ups and downs on people's lives will be.

At present, the battle for economic supremacy in the next generation is accelerating, involving the EU and the US, as well as Japan and China. Its symbol is the change in the automotive industry. The pandemic, and the economic turmoil that accompanies it, are compounding the ramifications of this struggle for supremacy.

界経済のリンクが進み始めた矢先のこの事件も、アメリカから瞬く間に世界に拡大しました。そして、そのパニックは**ファシスト政権の台頭**の一因ともなりました。そして世界大戦の結果、アメリカは世界最大最強の国家となったのです。

　今、世界が注意しなければならないこともこの3点、つまりパンデミックとそれによる不安定な経済状況、そして、激しさを増す次世代向けの自動車の開発競争かもしれません。

　技術革新のカーブが急坂になればなるほど、人々の生活を左右するパンデミックや株価の上下の影響も、これまで以上に迅速に波及し、深刻になります。

　今、EUとアメリカ、そして日本や中国を巻き込んで、次世代の経済への覇権争いが加速中です。そのシンボルが、自動車業界での変化です。パンデミックと、それに伴う経済の混乱が、この覇権争いにさらに複雑な影響を与えているのです。

第4章

Key word

HEGEMONY　覇権、ヘゲモニー

　「政治的、経済的、軍事的に一国あるいは一社会集団が他を支配・統制すること」を指します。本文では、次世代の自動車開発競争を通して、どの国が世界経済の覇権を握るのかということを述べています。2022年現在はGDP（国内総生産）ベースでアメリカと中国が覇権を争っていますが、いずれはそこに人口が世界第2位のインドが加わって、三つ巴の争いになるといわれています。自らの影響力を拡大させようと大国が他の国々に介入する覇権主義の傾向は、ウクライナに侵攻しているロシアをはじめ、東アジア・東南アジア・アフリカへの進出を目論んでいる中国など、顕著にみられるようになっています。今後の動向に要注目です。

例文

The US hegemony over international politics is beginning to waver.
国際政治におけるアメリカの覇権が揺らぎ始めている。

In this way, Hideyoshi established hegemony by 1590.
こうして秀吉は1590年までには覇権を確立した。

Interfering in the internal affairs of other countries and attempting to overthrow their regimes is hegemonic behavior.
他国の内政に干渉しその国の政権を転覆させようとすることは、覇権主義的な行動である。

 あなたはどう答える？

What is Japan's approach to electric vehicles and what is the current situation?
日本の電気自動車をめぐる取り組みと現状は？

ヒント 2035年までに乗用車の新車販売で電動車100％を目指していますが、電気自動車の販売比率は2.5％と伸び悩んでいます。政府は購入補助や充電インフラの整備を進めています。

覚えておくと便利な単語、表現

☐ **decarbonize the automobile**　自動車を脱炭素化する

☐ **develop infrastructure**　インフラを整備する

☐ **subsidize**　〔政府が〕補助金を払う

第18話
テスラはAIで次世代に挑戦する

Article 18
Tesla Challenges the Next Generation with AI

Tesla posts record net income of $438 million, revenue surges by 74%.

—— CNBC

（テスラは純利益で4億3800万ドルを〔2021年の第1四半期の〕決算として計上、収益は74％の急増となる）

Tesla's revenues are multiplying.

If you were told, "**innovation** in self-driving and electrification are inevitable challenges for the future of the automotive industry," you might say that everyone knows that. However, it should be noted that these things will have an impact far beyond the car business.

There is a term called "neural network." It indicates that by fostering a computer's ability to actually "see" things and **accumulate** experience, it will be possible for it to make various decisions based on its own vision.

Of the two challenges—creating driverless cars and electrifying them—Tesla has focused most on applying neural network innovations to the former.

Usually, to enable automated driving, supercomputers were used to store data representing actual roads, buildings, signs, etc. in three dimensions and **incorporate** these vast amounts of data into the car's functions. And as an **auxiliary function**, it was hoped that neural network technology could be used to steer and brake the car by looking at objects. It is very difficult for a computer to acquire the same vision as a human being. However, Tesla has attempted self-driving mainly with neural networks by means of a supercomputer called Dojo.

This means Tesla as a company is not simply an automaker **specializing in self-driving cars**. The technology behind Tesla is about to become a resource pool that will **foster** a new industry that goes beyond mere car manufacturing. Many American investors have **bitterly** criticized traditional Wall Street investors for

▶ innovation → p.176

　テスラが収益を急激に伸ばしています。

　「自動運転と電動化の**技術革新**は、今後の自動車業界にとって避けては通れない課題」だと言えば、誰もがそんなことはわかっていると思うかもしれません。しかし、この命題自体がすでに陳腐化していることに気がつくべきです。

　ニューラルネットワークという言葉があります。これはコンピュータの中に実際に物を見る能力を育て、その**経験を蓄積させる**ことで、コンピュータが自らの視覚によって様々な判断ができるようになることを示した言葉です。

　車の自動運転と電動化という課題のうち、前者におけるこのニューラルネットワークの技術革新に最も注力してきたのがテスラだったのです。

　通常、自動運転を可能にするには、スーパーコンピュータに実際の道路や建物、標識などを立体的に記憶させ、その車の機能にこれらの膨大なデータを**組み込む**方法がとられていました。そして、その**補助機能**として、物を見てハンドルやブレーキ操作を行うニューラルネットワークの技術があればと期待されていたのです。それほどまでに、コンピュータが人間と同じ視覚を獲得することは困難なのです。しかし、テスラはDojoというスーパーコンピュータによって、ニューラルネットワークを主体とした自動運転に挑んできたのです。

　このことは、テスラという企業が単に**自動運転に特化**した自動車メーカーではないということを意味します。テスラの背景にある技術は、単なる車の製造の域を超えた新しい産業を**育成する**プールになろうとしているのです。アメリカの多くの投資家は、ウォールストリートの伝

valuing Tesla solely as an automaker. Tesla is not a car company, but a company trying to **open up** a new field with AI. A new trend is emerging that is changing the very idea that automated driving can be completed only from within the automotive industry.

The housing market has long been used as an **indicator** of the economy's future. This is because when more houses are built, sold, and bought, the demand for various products, such as **home appliances**, increases, and the financial and health care industries also benefit from this. Similarly, automobiles and aircraft are at the top of a **wide range of** industries and, just like housing, have been used as a **benchmark** for a country's economy. However, the evaluation of the **core industries**, such as housing and automobiles, that support such an economy is now gradually changing. Tesla is the **epitome** of that. In other words, Tesla's growth has been made possible by AI solutions, such as Dojo.

To put it another way, the diverse technology firms in Silicon Valley and other places are not just **subcontracted** to manufacture a single product called a car, but are becoming positioned above it. Companies with such technology and intelligence are no longer parts manufacturers. The companies are about to take over as solution providers, as represented by neural network technology, becoming more important than houses and cars. Technologies and solutions supported by AI have created a wide variety of goods, and automobiles are about to become just one of those products.

統的な投資家が、あくまでもテスラを自動車会社として
しか評価してこなかったことを**痛烈**に批判しています。
テスラは自動車会社ではなく、AIで新分野を**切り開こう**
とする企業なのです。自動運転を自動車業界だけで完結
させようという発想自体を変えてゆく新たなトレンドが
生まれているのです。

　昔から経済の先行きを占うとき
に、住宅市場が**指標**に使われてきま
した。住宅の建設や売り買いが多く
なれば、そこに住む人の**家電**など
様々な製品の需要も伸び、金融や保
険業界までその恩恵を受けることが
できるからです。同様に自動車や航

空機は、**すそ野の広い産業**の頂点にあって、ちょうど住宅
のように、その国の経済を見る**基準**とされてきました。と
ころが、そんな経済を支える住宅や自動車といった**基幹
産業**への評価が、今少しずつ変わろうとしているのです。
テスラはその**象徴**と言えます。つまり、テスラがDojoな
どに代表されるAIのソリューションがあってこそ成長で
きたという事実を見れば明らかなのです。

　別の言い方をするならば、シリコンバレーなどにある
多様なテクノロジー企業が、車という単一の商品を製造
するための**下請け**ではなく、その上に位置するようにな
りつつあるのです。こうした技術や知能を持つ企業は、も
はや部品メーカーではありません。それらは、ニューラル
ネットワークの技術に代表されるようなソリューション
を与える企業として、住宅や自動車の上に君臨しようと
しているわけです。AIに支えられた技術やソリューショ
ンがあってこそ、多彩な商品が生み出され、自動車もそ
んな商品群の一つに過ぎなくなろうとしているのです。

第４章

Unless global automakers understand this and expand their innovation networks globally, they will not be able to develop new products. We need to look at the fact that the invisible accumulation of future technologies behind the creation of new cars, such as Teslas, is going to radically reshape the world in the future.

When it comes to the future of the automotive industry, it is impossible to achieve either without the **complementarity** and **integration** of automated driving technology and electrification know-how. Now Tesla is challenging itself to build a production base not only in the US, but also in Europe and China, and to develop an infrastructure network for electrification on the Eurasian continent. This can be compared to the telegraph poles that were needed when telegraph technology was born: AI technology solutions are changing the infrastructure itself **on a global scale.**

The US and China are currently locked in a fierce battle for supremacy in these technologies. More than territorial and military hegemony, AI technology hegemony has become the most important issue in international politics. The global industrial structure will dramatically change when automakers become subcontractors of AI solutions.

　世界の自動車メーカーも、こうした現実を理解し、イノベーションのネットワークを世界に拡大しない限り、新しい製品開発ができなくなります。テスラに代表される新しい自動車が生まれてくる背景にある、未来への見えない技術の集積が、これからの世界を操る黒幕であることに、目を向ける必要があるのです。

　自動車業界の未来について言うならば、自動運転の技術と電動化のノウハウがお互いに**補完**され、**融合**しなければ、そのどちらをも達成することは不可能です。今テスラはアメリカだけではなく、ヨーロッパや中国での生産拠点の構築を目指し、さらにユーラシア大陸での電動化のためのインフラネットワークを整備しようと挑戦しています。これは、ちょうど電信技術が生まれたときに建設が促進された電信柱にたとえられます。AI技術でのソリューションは、そうした**地球規模**でのインフラ自体を変化させようとしているのです。

　今、アメリカと中国はこうした技術での覇権をめぐって、つばぜり合いをしています。領土や軍事での覇権以上に、AI技術での覇権が国際政治の最も重要な課題となっているのです。自動車メーカーがAIソリューションの下請けになったとき、世界の産業構造は大きく変化してゆくはずです。

第4章

「テスラ」の社名の由来となった、電気技師で発明家のニコラ・テスラ。交流電流方式やリモコンを生み出したことで有名な彼に敬意を表してその名がつけられた

Key word

INNOVATION 革新、新機軸

　「既存のものや仕組みに対して新しい切り口から新たな価値を創造し、社会的に大きな変化をもたらすこと」です。日本ではこの一語で「技術革新」と訳されることが多いですが、この場合、英語ではtechnological innovationといいます。似たような言葉にinvention（発明）がありますが、こちらは「それまでに存在しなかったものや仕組みを新たに生み出すこと」です。つまり、最初の電話はinventionであり、最初の携帯電話はinventionもしくはinnovation、そして最初のスマートフォンはinnovationということができます。こうした革新をもたらす人、あるいは創意工夫に富む人のことをinnovatorといいます。

例文

Technological innovation brought about the rapid progress of the information industry.
技術革新は情報産業の飛躍的な発展をもたらした。

Language is one of the most important inventions of mankind.
言語は人類にとって最も重要な発明の一つである。

Steve Jobs was one of the best innovators in the United States.
スティーブ・ジョブズはアメリカで最も優れたイノベーターの一人だった。

あなたはどう答える？

How far has Japan's automated driving progressed?
日本の自動運転はどこまで進んでいますか？

 自動運転はレベル0から5までの6段階で示され、日本はハンズオフ運転が可能な2から自動運転初歩の3に移行しています。2020年4月から公道走行も可能になりました。

覚えておくと便利な単語、表現

☐ **be in an early phase of**　〜の初期段階にいる
☐ **drive with one's hands free**　手放しで運転する
☐ **street-legal vehicle**　公道を走れる車両

第19話
セミコンダクターの不足を鳥瞰すれば

Article 19
A Bird's-Eye View of
the Semiconductor Shortage

Today, millions of products—cars, washing machines, smartphones, and more—rely on computer chips, also known as semiconductors. And right now, there just aren't enough of them to meet industry demand. As a result, many popular products are in short supply.

—— BBC

（自動車から洗濯機、スマホに至るまで、数えきれない製品がセミコンダクター、つまりコンピュータ・チップに依存している。今、その供給が需要に追いつかず、人々が愛用する多くの製品の製造が滞っている）

Right now, the whole world is abuzz over the slowdown in the distribution of semiconductors.

Actually, this problem has nothing to do with the coronavirus pandemic. The **shortage of supply** in tiny chips which can fit on the tip of one's little finger that is shaking the world economy began even before the coronavirus spread throughout the world. Demand is rapidly **outstripping** supply.

In the age of 5G, the demand for chips is surging as the shift to AI continues.

Chips are used in everything from washing machines to televisions, from the refrigerator you open when you wake up for a glass of orange juice to the coffee maker you use to brew coffee. Moreover, everything from home appliances to cars and smartphones is being integrated and linked through the evolution of AI. Chips are the contact points that connect convenient functions, such as turning on the air conditioner before driving home in your car. In other words, a shortage of chips could overshadow the supply of the products that **form the basis of our lives**.

There is something we can learn from this **phenomenon**. It is a change in the way we think about the future of industry and even risk management. If we take the example of **futuristic** automobiles, which are complex and incorporate countless types of chips, it is said that the lack of just one chip and the inability to link it will **render all functions unusable**. Behind the fact that the world's major automobile manufacturers were forced to reduce their production volume targets by 2021, we can see how risk management failed to foresee the importance of a stable supply of the chips that underpin the pursuit of convenience.

► supply → p.184

　今、セミコンダクター（半導体）の流通が滞っていると
世界中が騒いでいます。

　実は、この問題はコロナのパンデミックとは無関係で
す。小指の上にすら置ける小さなチップの**供給不足**が世
界経済を揺るがす現象は、コロナが世界に拡散する前か
ら始まっていました。需要が供給を急速に上回ろうとし
ているのです。

　5Gの時代になり、AI化が進む中でチップの需要が急増
しています。

　朝起きてオレンジジュースを飲むために開ける冷蔵庫
や、コーヒーをいれるためのコーヒーメーカー、洗濯機
からテレビまで、ありとあらゆるところでチップは使わ
れています。しかも、こうした家電製品から自動車やス
マートフォンまでが、AIの進化によって一体化され、リ
ンクされようとしています。自家用車で帰宅する前に自
宅のエアコンをオンにすることが可能なように、利便性
がリンクする接点に常にチップが使用されているわけで
す。つまり、チップの不足は**我々の生活の基盤となる**製
品の供給にも影を落としかねないのです。

　この**現象**から見えてくることがあります。それは、これ
からの産業のあり方、さらにはリスクマネジメントに対
する考え方の変化です。数えきれないほどの種類のある
チップが複雑に組み込まれている未来型の自動車を例に
とれば、たった一つのチップが足りず、リンクしないだけ
で**すべての機能が使用不能になる**と言われています。世
界の主要な自動車メーカーが、2021年になって目標とし
た生産量を減らさざるを得なくなった背景には、こうし
た利便性を追求する下支えとなるチップの安定供給の重
要性を予見できなかったリスクマネジメントのあり方が

▶5Gとは「5th Generation」
の略称で、携帯電話などに
用いられる次世代通信規格
の5世代目を意味し、日本
語では「第5世代移動通信
システム」という。要件は①
高速大容量、②高信頼・低遅
延通信、③多数同時接続。

第4章

Initially, Japan was the largest supplier of semiconductors in the world. Now, Panasonic, Toshiba, and other companies have withdrawn from the industry, and their global market share has dropped to 6 percent. The winners, instead of Japan, were the US and Taiwan. Taiwan's TSMC, which has been in the news lately, has grown rapidly in the **contract manufacturing** of computer chips and has grown to account for 50 percent of the world's chip production, riding a **tailwind** from the trade war between the US and China that has hit Chinese manufacturers.

How this worked was simple. American semiconductor companies focused on design innovations in various areas that matched the **burgeoning** AI industry. Then, following their **blueprints**, Taiwan's TSMC would evolve manufacturing technologies that would allow for rapid customization and contract manufacturing. The cooperation between the two gave them a monopoly over computer chip production.

The **collaboration** between TSMC and American companies that develop computer chips is directly linked to the revival of the American automobile industry through automated driving and the expansion of initiatives in advanced technologies, such as biotechnology, which will give them an advantage over their Chinese rivals. Of course, the country that could benefit most from this strategy would be Taiwan. It would benefit its security to be firmly linked to the US economy.

In addition, as already explained, the current chip supply shortage is having a negative impact on American companies, such as Ford. However, **looking at the big picture**, when the supply of chips recovers in the future, the cooperation between the **development technology** of American semiconductors and

見え隠れするわけです。

　元々、世界で最も多くセミコンダクターを供給していたのは日本ですが、今ではパナソニックや東芝などがこの業界から撤退し、世界でのシェアは6％にまで落ち込んでいます。日本に代わって勝者となったのが、アメリカと台湾だったのです。最近とみに話題となっている台湾のTSMCは、コンピュータ・チップの**受託生産**で急成長し、アメリカと中国の貿易戦争によって中国のメーカーが打撃を受けたことによる**追い風**に乗って、世界のチップの生産の5割を占めるまでに大きくなったのです。

　この仕組みは簡単でした。アメリカのセミコンダクターの企業は、**躍進する**AI業界にマッチした様々な分野でのデザイン技術の革新に集中したのです。そして、その**設計図**に従って、台湾のTSMCはカスタムメイドに迅速に対応し、受託生産ができる製造技術を進化させます。この両者の協力によってコンピュータ・チップの生産の囲い込みが行われたのです。

　台湾のTSMCとアメリカのコンピュータ・チップを開発する企業との**連携**は、自動運転によるアメリカの自動車産業の復活や、バイオテクノロジーなどの先端技術でのイニシアチブを拡大させることに直結し、ライバルの中国に対して優位に立てるようになるわけです。もちろん、この戦略で最も利益を享受できたのは台湾でしょう。アメリカ経済としっかりとリンクすることは、台湾の安全保障にとっても有益なはずだからです。

　もちろん、すでに解説したように、今回のチップの供給不足はフォードなどのアメリカ企業にもマイナスの影響を与えています。しかし、**大局的に見る**ならば、今後チップの供給が回復したときに、アメリカのセミコンダクターの**開発技術**と、台湾の**生産技術**との連携は、ほと

第4章

the **production technology** of Taiwan should benefit almost all industries. Furthermore, the American semiconductor industry is constantly pursuing technological innovation through M&A and expanding its network around the world. Through M&A, technologies that belong to different organizations are fused and fermented.

What we have to learn from now on is exactly this M&A technique. It is important to be aware of M&A as a method of building a network for the next generation, rather than just positioning M&A as an **act of acquisition** to expand the company. In other words, it is necessary to change the mindset of **shareholders** in such a way that the pyramid-shaped thinking in which the buyer is at the top and the purchased company is at the bottom. Also, both sides must **circulate human resources** on an equal footing and obtain synergies through exchanges.

In other words, if companies can network with each other more flatly and casually, this will be the **shortest path** to technological innovation. Once this flat structure is in place, the ideas of these companies will be able to circulate and flow back into the world.

The challenges posed by a computer chip small enough to fit on one's little finger are having a profound impact on the future of global corporations.

んどすべての業界の利益となるはずです。さらに、アメリカのセミコンダクター業界は、常に技術革新を目指してM&Aを行い、世界にネットワークを拡大させています。M&Aによってそれぞれ異なった組織にあった技術が融合して発酵するわけです。

　これから学ばなければならないことは、まさにこのM&Aの技術です。M&Aを企業が膨張するための**買収行為**とだけ位置付けず、次世代に向けたネットワークの構築の手法として意識することが大切です。もっと言うならば、買う側が上で買われる側が下とするピラミッド型の発想をやめ、双方が対等に**人材を還流させ**、交流によるシナジーを得るよう**株主の意識を変革させる**必要があるのです。

　つまり、企業同士がよりフラットでカジュアルにネットワークできれば、それが技術革新に向かう**最短の道へ**とつながるのです。このフラットな仕組みづくりさえできれば、その企業の発想が再び世界に流通し還流するようになるはずです。
　小指にのるほどのコンピュータ・チップのもたらした課題は、今後のグローバル企業のあり方にも大きな影響を与えているのです。

第4章

Key word

SUPPLY 供給、供給する

　supply「供給」の対義語「需要」はdemandです。本文では、需要が急増している半導体（semiconductor）の供給不足（shortage of supply）という現象を通して、産業構造や組織のあり方についての課題を考察しています。名詞は複数形のsuppliesで「生活必需品」という意味も表します。関連して覚えておきたい言葉は「サプライチェーン（supply chain）」です。製品の原材料・部品の調達から、製造、在庫管理、配送、販売を経て、消費者の手に届くまでの全体の一連の流れのことで、日本語では「供給連鎖」ともいわれます。半導体不足によって、このサプライチェーン・マネジメントの重要性が改めて問われているのです。

例文

Prices rise when demand exceeds supply.
需要が供給を上回ると価格は上昇する。

Our shelters do not have enough relief supplies.
私たちの避難所には十分な救援物資がない。

The shortage of semiconductors has rocked our company's supply chain.
半導体の供給不足は、当社のサプライチェーンを揺るがした。

❓ あなたはどう答える？

How is Japan coping with the shortage of semiconductors?
日本では半導体不足にどのように対応していますか？

ヒント TSMC熊本工場の建設、トヨタやデンソーなど8社が出資する新会社の設立、半導体の研究開発や生産整備への政府予算充当など、官民で半導体産業の立て直しを図っています。

覚えておくと便利な単語、表現

☐ **appropriate a government budget for** 〜に政府予算を充てる
☐ **both the public and private sectors** 官民ともに
☐ **revitalize the industry** 産業を再生させる

第20話
ナリウッドに象徴される
グローバルな人材交流

Article 20
Global Talent Exchange Symbolized by
Nollywood and Others

Nollywood is another industry that seems to be passing Hollywood in terms of the amount of movies it produces a year.

—— StudioBinder

（ナリウッドは年間映画制作本数において、ハリウッドを抜くもう一つの映画産業だ）

Today, there is a growing dispersion in the global entertainment industry.

Initially, the entertainment industry was centered in Hollywood and New York. However, in the 21st century, as represented by K-POP, which has expanded from South Korea to the rest of the world, various regions are competing with each other and beginning to challenge the global market, aided by social media and other means.

Taking Africa as an example, Nigeria is now **attracting attention**.

It is the center of the African film industry. Just as Mumbai (formerly Bombay), India, is the film hub of South Asia and is called Bollywood after Hollywood, Nigeria is challenging the global film industry under the name Nollywood.

In Lagos, Nigeria's largest industrial city, numerous productions are **underway**, attracting film professionals from neighboring countries, such as Senegal and Cameroon. In terms of the number of productions, it is the second largest in the world. The number of films produced annually is a whopping 2,500. Incidentally, the current statistics show that Bollywood is in first place, and Hollywood, the original home of movie production, is after Nigeria.

Lagos produces mainly regular **entertainment films**, not musical-style ones like Bollywood does. Sometimes it collaborates with the United Arab Emirates (UAE) and other countries to produce these films.

What is interesting when talking to actors working in Nollywood is that they are **extremely fluent** in English, although

　今、世界のエンターテインメント業界での分散が進んでいます。

　元々エンターテインメント産業といえば、アメリカのハリウッドやニューヨークが中心でした。しかし21世紀になって、韓国から世界に拡大したK-POPに代表されるように、世界各地がそれぞれ競いながら、SNSなども手伝ってグローバルな市場への挑戦を始めています。

　アフリカを例に取ってみると、**注目されている**のはナイジェリアです。

　ナイジェリアはアフリカの映画産業の中心地なのです。インドのムンバイ（旧称ボンベイ）が南アジアの映画のハブで、ハリウッドになぞらえてボリウッドと呼ばれているように、ナイジェリアは「ナリウッド」の名前で世界の映画界に挑戦しているのです。

　ナイジェリア最大の産業都市ラゴスでは、セネガルやカメルーンなどの隣国からも映画関係者が集まって、数多くのプロダクションが**進行中**です。実は制作数でいうと、世界第2位の規模となっています。年間の制作数はなんと2500本。ちなみに第1位はボリウッドで、本家本元のハリウッドはナイジェリアの次点というのが現在の統計です。

　ラゴスでは、ボリウッドのようなミュージカル風の映画ではなく、通常の**娯楽映画**を中心に制作しています。時には、アラブ首長国連邦などともコラボして制作を進めています。

　ナリウッドで活動する役者と話をしてみて興味深いのは、アフリカ独特のアクセントはあるものの、英語が**極**

第4章

ラゴス

they have a distinctly African accent. This is also true, for example, in Uganda, in the central part of Africa, which is attracting attention as a new source of online English teachers. The fact that both Nigeria and Uganda were originally British colonies is expected to lead to the growth of these new English-speaking markets.

A network of **former British colonies** that gained independence 60 to 80 years ago is now beginning to communicate to the world in the common language of English.

One actress working in Nollywood frequently flies from Lagos to Dubai to work on film productions there. Then, she sometimes goes straight to the US to work.

It is likely that more and more Nollywood actors and actresses will have agents in both the Middle East and the US to expand their activities in the future. In fact, Nollywood was born as a source of films for Africa, and its quality and content were not high in the beginning. However, in the late 1990s, Nollywood **caught the attention** of the international film industry and was subsequently introduced in the New York Times and other publications. It was not until the turn of the century that the film industry officially began to grow with investment. This is due to the fact that the way people connect has changed dramatically with the establishment of the internet. **Recruitment** is now global, and people working in Nollywood can expand their recruiting opportunities worldwide.

Needless to say, the world of professional sports and show business in the US is taking notice of this trend. As long as you have an interpreter, reaching out to and negotiating with talented

▶ recruit → p.192

めて**流暢**なことです。このことは、例えばアフリカの中央部にあるウガンダなどでも言えることで、ウガンダの場合は、オンライン英会話教師の新たな供給源として注目されているのです。ナイジェリアにしてもウガンダにしても、元々イギリスの植民地であったことが、こうした新たな英語を使ったマーケットへの成長につながると期待されているのです。

　60年から80年前に独立した**旧イギリス領**のネットワークが、今英語という共通の言語で世界に向けた発信を始めていることになります。

　ナリウッドで活動するある女優は、頻繁にラゴスからドバイに飛び、そこで映画のプロダクションに携わっています。そして、そのままアメリカで仕事をすることもあるようです。

　今後、中東とアメリカの双方にエージェントを持ち、活動の舞台を広げてゆこうとするケースが増えてゆきそうです。実のところ、ナリウッドはアフリカへの映画の供給源として誕生しましたが、当初はその質もコンテンツも決してよいものではありませんでした。それが、1990年代の終わりごろに海外の映画界の**目にとまり**、その後ニューヨーク・タイムズなどでも紹介されました。次第に投資も集まり、映画産業として正式に成長を始めたのは今世紀に入ってからのことだったのです。背景にはインターネットの定着によって、人々のつながり方が大きく変化していることが挙げられます。今、人材の**リクルート**は世界規模で、ナリウッドで働く人々もリクルートのチャンスを世界に拡大できるようになったのです。

　こうした動きに注目しているのが、アメリカのプロスポーツやショービジネスの世界であることは言うまでもありません。通訳さえいれば、有能な人材に声をかけて

映画撮影（イメージ）

第4章

people is not difficult.

Even more remarkable is that this network of recruiters is not limited to such special fields as the movie and baseball businesses, but is spread throughout all kinds of industries.

Even when planning a new business, it has become commonplace for companies to recruit from each other and exchange professionals, such as talented engineers from overseas.

In the future, it will be difficult for the **human resources market** to function within the **confines** of a single country. This is because the **hollowing out of occupations** due to the introduction of AI is expected to exceed the curve of population decline.

If you're looking for a job just to feed yourself, without thinking about your purpose in life, there may still be jobs available. However, if you are looking for a **rewarding job**, the supply of people who can earn enough money to sustain themselves for the rest of their lives without worrying about their livelihoods may well **exceed** the actual demand in a single country in the future.

The cost of film production in Nollywood is lower than in the US. Taking advantage of this price difference, production may be outsourced. At the same time, there are more opportunities for people who succeed in such markets to go out into the world as higher-priced talent.

交渉をすることはそれほど困難なことではないのです。

　さらに注目したいのは、こうしたリクルートのネットワークが映画界や野球界といったような特別な場所だけで行われているのではなく、ありとあらゆる産業の中に拡散している現実です。

　新しいビジネスを企画するときですら、海外の優秀な技術者などと交流し、お互いにリクルートし合うことも当たり前のことになってきています。

　これからの**人材市場**は、一つの国だけの**閉ざされた**マーケットでは機能しにくくなるでしょう。というのも、人口減少のカーブ以上に、AI化などによる**職業の空洞化**が予測されるからです。

　生きがいを考えずに、食べるためだけに職を求めるなら、まだ求人はあるかもしれません。しかし、**やりがいのある仕事**という条件で考えたとき、充分な収入を得て、生活に不安を持たずに一生を維持してゆくための人材の供給が、一つの国の中だけでは実際の需要を**上回る**ことが将来十分に考えられるのです。

　ナリウッドでの映画の制作費用はアメリカに比べれば安価です。こうした価格差を活用した制作のアウトソースも進んでゆくかもしれません。同時に、そうした市場で成功した才能ある人が、より高価な人材として世界に羽ばたくチャンスも増えているのです。

第4章

Key word

RECRUIT　募集［採用］する

　名詞形で「新入社員、新メンバー」も意味します。元々の意味は「軍隊に兵士を採用［補充］する」ことです。日本語でも某人材ビジネス企業の名前に使われていたり、就職活動時に着用する「リクルートスーツ」という言葉があったりしますね。

　日本の雇用慣行は海外では見られない独自性があります。その代表的なものが、終身雇用・年功序列賃金・新卒一括採用です。企業にとっては毎年計画的に人材を採用できるメリットがありますが、新卒・既卒・中途の機会不均等や正規・非正規の賃金格差などの問題も指摘される中、優秀な人材は海外に流出するなどしており、激化する世界的な人材獲得競争への対応を迫られています。

例文

The company is recruiting employees for a new project.
その企業は新しいプロジェクトのために社員を募集している。

The new recruit was late on his first day at the company.
その新入社員は入社初日に遅刻してきた。

The captain exercised the new recruits with long marches.
隊長は長時間行軍させて新兵たちを訓練した。

❓ あなたはどう答える？

Please tell us about the Japanese entertainment industry.
日本のエンターテインメント産業について教えてください。

> **ヒント**　産業の大半を映像・ゲーム分野が占め、この10年ではゲーム・キャラクター事業が伸長、出版は縮小の一途です。またデジタル市場が3割を占め、さらに拡大し続けています。

覚えておくと便利な単語、表現

☐ consist mostly of　〜が大半を占める
☐ declining publishing industry　衰退する出版業界
☐ expand the market　市場を拡大させる

第 5 章

世界から見た日本

Chapter 5

Japan from a Global Perspective

第21話
安倍元首相銃撃事件から見える
日本人の意識

Article 21
Japanese Attitudes Seen in the Shooting of
Former Prime Minister Abe

Japan had only one gun related death reported in 2021
—— CNN

（日本では2021年に銃に関連した死亡事案はたった1件しか起きていなかった）

Various **media outlets** are providing commentary on the shooting of former Prime Minister Abe. However, one cannot help but feel that all of them seem to be missing one important point regarding Japan's problems.

When the incident occurred, the foreign media reported the progression of events in real time. When the former prime minister died a little after 5:00 p.m., the BBC and other media changed the wording from "shot" to "assassinated" at that moment, reporting the **ever-changing** situation at exactly the same speed as NHK and other media.

In the midst of this, an **anchor** from one of the major American media outlets said to a Japanese **correspondent** suspiciously, "It seems to me that there is very little **security**." The correspondent responded that this was because Japanese elections emphasize contact between voters and candidates, and that strict **gun controls** mean that terrorist acts involving guns are rarely to be anticipated.

The issue of gun control has become a serious political issue in the US due to the frequency of shootings. Therefore, ironically, it was apparent that the American media intended to use the tragedy in Japan to convey the seriousness of the gun issue in the US by explaining how few gun crimes there are in Japan and that this incident is an unusual situation, rather than the other way around.

Also, with regard to messages of **condolence** from governments, prime ministers, and others, the first word that stood out was "shocked," i.e., expressing shock at the news of this incident. It was also explained that they were expressing their "shock" at the fact that such a thing could happen even in Japan.

▶ security → p.202

　安倍元首相が銃撃された事件について、いろいろな**マ
スコミ**が解説をしています。しかし、どの解説をとって
も1点だけ、大切な日本の課題についてのコメントが抜け
ているような気がしてならないのです。
　事件が起きたとき、海外のメディアはリアルタイムで
その経過を報道していました。午後5時過ぎに元首相が亡
くなったときも、その瞬間にBBCなどのテロップが「銃
撃」から「暗殺」へと表現が変わり、NHKなどと全く同
じ早さで**刻々と変化する**状況が伝えられていました。

　その中で、アメリカのある主要メディアの**キャスター**
が、日本の**特派員**に対して「**警備**がほとんどないように
見えるのですが」と怪訝な顔をして質問しました。それ
に対して特派員は、日本の選挙が有権者と候補者とが触
れ合うことを重視していて、かつ**銃規制**が厳しいことも
あり、銃によるテロ行為をほとんど想定していないから
だと答えていました。
　アメリカでは銃乱射事件が頻発し、銃規制の問題が深
刻な政治課題になっています。したがって、皮肉なこと
に、アメリカのメディアは日本での惨劇を利用して、い
かに日本での銃の犯罪が少なく、この事件が異常な事態
なのかという解説によって、逆にアメリカの銃の課題の
深刻さを伝えようとする意図が見えていました。

▶アメリカで複数の犠牲者
が出た銃乱射事件は増加傾
向にあり、2020年から2022
年は3年連続で年600件以
上も発生している。単純計
算で1日に約1.64件だが、多
いときにはひと月で60件
以上も起きている。（出典：
Gun Violence Archive）

第5章

　また、各国の政府や首相などからの**哀悼**のメッセージ
についても、最初に「shocked」、つまりこの事件の報
道を受けてショックを受けているという表現が目立ちま
した。そのことについても、日本ですらこんなことが起
きるのかということへの「ショック」を表明したのだと

Soon, in response to the reactions of the foreign media, people in Japan began to question whether security was **sufficient**, and some criticized the response of the Nara Prefectural Police and other authorities.

However, amidst this trend, one can sense one idea that is common among Japanese people. That is the feeling that what is happening in the world is happening in other countries, and that such a thing will not happen in Japan.

The **essence** of this incident is that Japanese people fundamentally lack the awareness that what happens in the world can also happen in Japan.

Certainly, the situation in Japan is not like in the US, where gun violence causes chaos in society. It is also true that gun control in Japan is extremely strictly enforced compared with the rest of the world. However, shootings of politicians have occurred in Japan, and in 2007, the then-mayor of Nagasaki was shot and killed.

Fortunately, there have been no bombings like those in the Middle East so far, but many people may even have forgotten the fact that a large number of subway riders were killed or injured in the Sarin gas incident caused by Aum Shinrikyo. If a former prime minister can be assassinated with a **homemade** gun, there is nothing to guarantee that a homemade bomb will not be used in a terrorist attack. In other words, the incident made us realize that the myth that Japan, unlike other countries, is "safe and convenient" is simply an **unfounded conceit.**

In addition, in the case of a former prime minister, he or she has access to national and diplomatic secrets, and it is an international norm that security for such people is strictly enforced

解説されていました。

　やがて、海外メディアの反応を受けて、日本でも警備が**充分**だったのかと疑問視する指摘が出始め、奈良県警などの対応への批判の声も上がりました。

　しかし、こうした流れの中で、日本人に共通している1つの意識を感じます。それは、世界で起きていることは他所の国のことで、日本でそんなことは起きないだろうという気持ちです。

　世界で起きていることは日本でも起こり得るという意識が、日本人には根本的に欠如していることが、今回の事件の**本質**ではないでしょうか。

　確かに、アメリカのように銃の乱射が社会を混乱させるような状況は、日本にはありません。また、日本の銃規制は世界の中でも極めて厳しく実施されているのも事実です。しかし、日本でも政治家への銃撃は起きていますし、2007年には当時の長崎市長が射殺されています。

　幸い、中東で起きているような爆弾テロ事件は今のところありませんが、オウム真理教によるサリンガス事件で地下鉄利用者の多くが犠牲者・負傷者となった事実すら忘れてしまっている人も多いのではないでしょうか。**手製の銃**で首相経験者が暗殺されるのであれば、手製の爆弾でテロが起きないことを保証するものは何もないはずです。つまり、日本は他と違って「安全で便利な国だ」という神話が、単なる**根拠のない自惚れ**だということを我々に突きつけたのが、この事件だったのです。

　また、首相経験者のような人物の場合、国や外交の機密に触れているわけで、こうした人々への警備はどのような事情であれ、徹底されるのが国際的な常識でもあり

▶地下鉄サリン事件は1995年3月20日（月）午前8時ごろ、丸ノ内線・日比谷線・千代田線の地下鉄車両内で化学兵器として使用される神経ガスのサリンが散布された無差別テロ事件。

under any circumstances.

In fact, this "Japan is different" mentality is one of our most serious problems.

When companies explain the Japanese market to overseas suppliers and others, we often hear comments such as, "The Japanese market is unique," or "Japanese **consumers** are special and **fussy about details**." It is true that there is a difference between the perceptions of Japanese consumers and those of consumers in other countries. What is important, however, is to be aware that every market is unique and that every consumer, no matter where he or she is, has his or her own unique needs. Japan is not the only market that is different from others; every market has its own unique **characteristics**.

There is a link between this idea of "Japan is unique" and the idea of "Japan is safe." In other words, we need to be aware that Japan is not the only **exception**.

If Japan's foreign policy is to cooperate with the rest of the world in dealing with terrorism and barbaric acts such as Russia's invasion of Ukraine, we must first change this missing awareness.

ます。

　実はこの「日本は違う」という意識は、我々の深刻な
病巣の1つです。

　企業が海外のサプライヤーなどに日本の市場について
説明するとき、「日本の市場はユニークなんです」、「日本
の**消費者**は特別で、**細かいことにうるさいんです**」とい
ったコメントをよく耳にします。確かに日本の消費者の
感覚と、諸外国の消費者の意識には違うものがあるでし
ょう。しかし、大切なことは、どこの市場もそれぞれに
ユニークであり、どこの消費者であっても、それぞれに
独自のニーズを持っているという意識です。日本だけが
他と違っているのではなく、どこも同様にそれぞれの**特
色**があるのです。

　この「日本は特殊」という意識と「日本は安全」という
意識には、リンクするところがあります。つまり、日本
だけが**例外**ではないのだということを、我々はしっかり
と意識しておく必要があるのです。

　世界と協調して、テロリズムやロシアによるウクライ
ナ侵攻のような蛮行に対応するのが日本の外交方針であ
るならば、こうした欠落した意識そのものを、まずは変
えてゆかなければならないのではないでしょうか。

第5章

Key word

SECURITY 安全、警備

「危険や恐れのない状態」あるいは「犯罪や攻撃を防ぐために講じる措置」のことを表す名詞です。形容詞ではsecureやsafeを使って同じような「安全な、不安のない」状態を表します。

本文では銃犯罪の多いアメリカから見ればかなり手薄だった事件当時の警備は、「日本は安全だ」「日本で銃犯罪など起きるわけない」という日本人の意識からだったのではないかと考察しています。日本が世界と協調して情勢を考えていくうえで、日本だけが特別だという意識から、どこの国もそれぞれに特色があり日本も同じことが起こりうるのだという意識へと変わっていく必要があるのです。

例文

Military security has been stepped up since the recent uprising.
今回の暴動以来、軍事的な警備が強化されている。

Do you feel secure about the future?
将来について不安はありませんか？

There is no country in the world that is safe from attack.
世界には攻撃されない国はない。

あなたはどう答える？

What are the challenges of counterterrorism in Japan?
日本におけるテロ対策の課題は何でしょうか？

ヒント 情報収集に特化した機関や制度、サイバー空間での思想の伝播やテロへの対応、各国の治安情報機関との連携など、諸外国の組織や制度を調べたうえで考えてみましょう。

覚えておくと便利な単語、表現

☐ **intelligence agency** 情報機関
☐ **protect important people** 要人を警護する
☐ **rarely to be anticipated** 想定外の

第22話
ゴッホとイーロン・マスク
──2人から見たイノベーションの本質

Article 22
Van Gogh and Elon Musk—The Essence of
Innovation from Their Point of View

Elon Musk reportedly secretly welcomed twins with a top executive just weeks before his baby with Grimes was born last year

—— BuzzFeed News

（イーロン・マスクはグライムスとの間に子どもが生まれる数週間前に、自らの会社の重役との間に密かに双子をもうけていたことが判明）

What would you do if the famous Van Gogh lived next door?

If you ask that question, many people would probably answer, "I'd call the police." He is none other than the **eccentric** who cut off his own ear, chased Gauguin around, and created wondrous works of art in a room stained with paint.

Mysterious artworks—that's right. Has anyone ever **taken a step back** and thought for themselves whether his **masterpieces**, such as *Cypresses* and *Sunflowers*, are truly amazing works of art? Few people could have been convinced when they saw them, not in a museum, but unframed in his **dingy** room, that they would be the ones to attract art lovers around the world in the future. The same would be true if Van Gogh were to appear before our eyes today.

He **boldly** challenged the conventional wisdom of beauty, changing it and passing it on to future generations.

Or what would you do if Steve Jobs were with you?

He certainly changed the world. However, it was common for him to use power harassment, such as **verbally abusing** employees who did not agree with him. In his younger days, he hated taking baths and would come to meetings with bankers and other people wearing sandals and shorts, with a strong body odor. **Inconsistency** was an everyday occurrence, and many people hated him because he tended to assume things and had an idiosyncratic **personality**.

So what about Elon Musk? What would you think if you knew about his personal life?

He caused a **huge uproar** when it was revealed that he

▶ personality → p.210

　もし、あのゴッホが隣に住んでいたら、あなたはどうしますか？

　そう問いかけると、多くの人がおそらく「警察に通報する」と答えるかもしれません。彼は、自らの耳を切ってゴーギャンを追いかけ回し、絵の具で汚れた部屋の中で不可思議な作品を創っている奇人に他なりません。

包帯をしてパイプをくわえた自画像

　不可思議な作品――そうです。「糸杉」や「ひまわり」といった彼の名作が本当にすごい作品なのか、一歩引いて自分の頭で考えた人はいるでしょうか。美術館ではなく、彼の薄汚れた部屋で、しかも額縁にも入っていない作品を見たとき、それが将来、世界中の美術愛好家を魅了するものになると確信を持てた人は少なかったはずです。そして、今目の前にゴッホが現れても同じことでしょう。

　しかし、彼は美というものへの常識にも果敢にチャレンジし、常識そのものを変え、後世につなぎました。

　それなら、スティーブ・ジョブズがあなたのそばにいたら、どうするでしょうか？

　彼は確かに世界を変えました。しかし、意に沿わない社員を言葉汚く罵るなど、パワハラは当たり前のこと。若い頃はお風呂嫌いで、強い体臭を撒き散らしながら、サンダルに短パン姿で銀行家などとの会合にもやってきました。朝令暮改は日常のことで、思い込みが強く、その強い個性に翻弄され、彼を憎んだ人も数多くいたようです。

　では、イーロン・マスクは？　もしあなたが彼のプライベートな生活を知ったらどう思うでしょうか。

　Google創業者の妻との不倫が暴かれ大騒動。その前に

had an affair with the wife of Google's founder. Before that, he had twins with an executive at the company he runs, and when confronted about violating the **company's code of ethics**, he reiterated that he was helping to curb the declining birthrate. Moreover, he is also in a relationship with another woman and had a baby boy with a musician named Grimes at approximately the same time. He is not a man who can be evaluated by normal moral standards.

The list of such eccentricities and insane episodes involving people who have changed the world is endless. And many people **tolerate** such behavior, saying that they are exceptions because they are geniuses.

But what would you do if such a person was actually your neighbor or **colleague**?

None of these actions should be tolerated. But it is also true that their strong personalities are the **driving force** that will create the future the world needs. The numerous scandals surrounding Elon Musk also violated the code of ethics of the organizations with which he himself was associated. But it is also true that punishing him for that would be a loss for the future of the automobile industry, space exploration, and many other fields.

Let us now turn our attention to those who work in Japanese companies today.

If Elon Musk or Steve Jobs came to a Japanese company, what would it look like in their eyes? Seeing as the people working there are extremely **obedient** to common sense and organization while suppressing their individuality, it seems likely they would criticize and pour every possible abuse on them. And what if

は、自らが経営する会社の重役との間に双子の子どもを
もうけ、**社内倫理規定**に違反していると突っ込まれると、
少子化問題に歯止めをかけるのに貢献しているんだ、と
開き直る始末。しかも、他の女性との関係も同時進行で、
グライムスというミュージシャンとの間にもほぼ同時に
男児をもうけています。通常のモラルで彼を評価するこ
とができるものではありません。

　世界を変えた人たちにまつわるこうした奇行、非常識
なエピソードをあげれば、きりがありません。そして、多
くの人は、彼らは天才だから例外だといって、そうした
行動を**容認**します。
　しかし、そんな人が本当にあなたの隣人であったり、
会社の**同僚**だったりしたら、あなたはどうするでしょう
か？
　これらの行為すべてを容認はできないはずです。しか
し、彼らの強い個性こそが世界に求められる将来を創る
原動力になることも事実です。イーロン・マスクをめぐ
る数々のスキャンダルは、彼自身が関係する組織の倫理
規定にも抵触していました。しかし、そのことで彼を葬
り去れば、今後の自動車業界、宇宙開発など様々な分野
での損失になることも事実でしょう。

　ここで、今の日本企業で働く人に目を向けてみましょ
う。
　もし日本企業にイーロン・マスクやスティーブ・ジョ
ブズがやってきたら、彼らの目にはどのように映るでし
ょうか？　そこで働いている、個性を抑え常識と組織に
極めて**従順**な人たちを見て、きっと言葉の限りの罵声を
浴びせ、批判するのではないでしょうか。そして、もし

第5章

someone like Van Gogh joined the company as a new employee?

The theme here is that innovation requires a strong personality. Strong personalities may create conflicts with company or organizational compliance regulations. Of course, there is an argument that people who are **unfamiliar with** the organization should work hard outside it. However, am I the only one who thinks that in today's society, everything has become a huge organization, inhibiting such individuality, and suppressing talent with cut-rate common sense? As someone who has seen many cases in which many brains have been **drained** from Japan, or people who came to Japan **with a yearning** for traditional Japanese culture have left disappointed, I fear that the cause of these things is the lack of individuality and **averageness** in Japanese society as a whole.

Nothing will come from **appreciating** the unique works of our predecessors in museums simply because they are famous works from textbooks. From our point of view, they are unique individuals. However, when their individuality breaks down the door to the future, the artists themselves may have been unaware of such a fact and simply painted their works in silence, or they may have suffered from unhelpful **alienation**, loneliness, and mental conflicts, or were **shunned** by the people around them.

If you remove the frames, that is, if you look at such works of art without any **preconceptions**, you may see a completely different aspect of the work.

Van Gogh and Elon Musk. It seems to me that we need to incorporate the thread that connects these two men into Japanese society and once again consider what innovation and human resources are all about.

ゴッホのような人が新入社員として入社し
てきたらどうでしょうか？

　ここで問いかけたいのは、イノベーショ
ンには強い個性が必要だというテーマで
す。強い個性は会社や組織のコンプライア
ンス規定との対立を生み出すかもしれません。組織に**馴
染めない人**は、組織の外で頑張るべきだという議論も当
然あるでしょう。しかし、今の社会は、社会全体が巨大
な組織となって、そうした個性を阻害し、安価な常識の
刃で才能の芽を摘み取っているように思えるのは、私一
人でしょうか。日本から多くの頭脳が**流出**したり、せっ
かく日本の伝統文化に**憧れて**来日してきた人が失望をも
って日本から離れていったりしたケースを何度も見てき
た者としては、その原因が、日本社会全体の没個性と**平
均化**にあるのではないかと、危惧してしまうのです。

　美術館で先人たちの個性ある作品をただ教科書に載っ
ている有名な作品だからといって**鑑賞**しても、そこから
は何も生まれません。彼らは我々から見れば変わった個
性の持ち主です。しかし、その個性が未来へのドアを突き
破るとき、作家本人はそんな事実も意識せず、ただ黙々
と作品を描いていたか、あるいは助けようのない**疎外感**
や孤独、そして精神的な葛藤に悶えて、周囲から**遠巻き
にされ**、突き放されていたかもしれません。

　額縁を除去して、つまり、**先入観**を外してそうした作
品をしっかりと鑑賞すると、そこに全く別の作品の顔が
見えてくることもあるはずです。

　ゴッホとイーロン・マスク。この2人をつなぐ糸を日本
の社会に組み入れて、もう一度イノベーションとは、そ
して人材とは何かということを考えてみる必要があるよ
うに思えるのです。

第5章

Key word

PERSONALITY 個性、性格

　この単語が主に表しているのは「〔ある人の性質や状態を表す〕性格、人となり」です。それがその人の「魅力、個性」になります。本文では idiosyncratic personality（独特な性格）、strong personality（強い個性）のように使われています。他に individuality という単語もでてきますが、これは「〔他の人と異なる、その人特有の〕人格、個性」で、社会的集団と対比させた「個別性」という意味も表します。さらに unique works（個性ある作品）、unique individual（変わった個性の持ち主）のように、形容詞 unique（唯一無二の、独特の）を使って「個性」を表すこともできます。

. . . .

例文

My nephew has a nice personality.
私の甥っ子は性格がいい。

In Japan, people are expected to suppress their individuality and fit in with the group.
日本では個性を抑えて集団に合わせることが求められる。

His sensibility was unique and absolutely amazing.
彼の感性は独特で、本当に素晴らしいものだった。

？ あなたはどう答える？

How can innovation and strong individuality be compatible in Japanese society?
イノベーションと強い個性を日本社会で両立させるには？

> **ヒント** あなたの同僚や隣人にゴッホやジョブズ、マスクがいたらと想像してください。彼らがあなたや組織にもたらす利点と欠点を検討して、どうしたらよいか考えてみましょう。

覚えておくと便利な単語、表現

☐ **consider the advantages and disadvantages** 　利点と欠点を検討する

☐ **embrace** 〔主義・思想などを〕受け入れる

☐ **inclusive society** 　共生社会

第23話
「日本人の心」を静かにアピールした
キャディの一礼

Article 23
The Quiet Appeal of the "Japanese Spirit" in a Caddie's Bow

Golf fans loved Hideki Matsuyama's caddie bowing to the course after historic Masters win

—— USA Today

（ゴルフファンはマスターズでの歴史的な快挙後の、松山英樹のキャディの一礼に心を打たれている）

When Hideki Matsuyama won the Masters, one thing in particular caught people's attention. It was when his caddie, Mr. Hayafuji, took off his cap and **bowed** to the course, which had regained its **serenity** after the match was over. The scene was viewed nearly 2 million times on YouTube and other sites, and the American press covered the scene more than they paid tribute to Matsuyama.

A golf course is just a golf course once the game is over. But the act of showing respect to such a place after the match is over is **very new** to people overseas. In a sense, Mr. Hayafuji's act may be quite natural for Japanese people. However, the act of expressing **gratitude** and respect for "things" and "places" is a **traditional value** unique to Japan.

Recently, it has been said that Japanese values are being lost. Japanese people now express their joy by raising their voices and **doing a fist-pump** when they win a game, and they express their joy, anger, sorrow, and pleasure more frankly than before. The incomprehensible communication style of the Japanese, which has been criticized by people overseas as representing "the **vague** Japanese" or "the **inscrutable** Japanese," is probably changing.

However, I believe that Hayafuji's act, although it only lasted for a few seconds, left something significant in the hearts of people around the world. As shown in the video from the American sports network ESPN, it was very impressive to see him standing alone and bowing to the 18th hole when all the people, including Matsuyama, who had **won the fierce battle**, had moved to the place of celebration and there was no one else left there.

Watching the media reaction, I now want to think again

　松山英樹選手がマスターズを制したとき、特に注目されたことがあります。それはキャディの早藤さんが、試合が終わって**静けさを取り戻した**コースに向かって、帽子をとって**一礼**してその場を去ったことでした。この模様がYouTubeなどで200万回近く閲覧され、アメリカのマスコミも松山選手への賛辞以上にこの光景を取り上げました。

一礼する早藤さん
（動画キャプチャ）

　ゴルフコースは試合が終わってしまえば、ただのゴルフ場です。でも、そんな場所に試合が終わったあと敬意を示す行為は、海外の人には**とても新鮮**です。ある意味では早藤さんの行為は、日本人にとっては至極当たり前のことかもしれません。しかし、「もの」や「場所」に**感謝や敬意を伝える行為**は、日本ならではの**伝統的な価値観**なのです。

　最近、日本の価値観が失われつつあると言われています。日本人は試合に勝てば声をあげて**ガッツポーズ**で喜びを表現し、喜怒哀楽を以前より率直に表現するようになりました。海外の人から「**曖昧な日本人**」とか「**不可解な日本人**」と批判されてきた、日本人のわかりにくいコミュニケーションスタイルが変わってきているのでしょう。

　しかし、今回の早藤キャディの行為は、ほんの数秒間のことでありながら、世界中の人の心に何か大きなものを残してくれたと思います。アメリカのスポーツ専門メディア ESPN の動画にあるとおり、**激戦を制した**松山選手などすべての人が祝福の場所へ移動し、誰もいなくなった18番ホールに、彼が一人立って一礼している姿がとても印象的だったのです。

　そんなメディアの反応を見ながら、日本人の伝統的な

about how we can positively **convey** the traditional values of the Japanese people to those overseas. Indeed, it has been said that Japanese people are among the most difficult people in the world to communicate with, because of their weak eye contact, **modest** gestures, and tendency to be **reticent**, which is partly because of their limited English ability.

On the other hand, we cannot ignore the fact that Japanese values have been favorably accepted, as evidenced by the use of the word "mottainai," which symbolizes the Japanese culture of valuing things, at the United Nations, and the best-selling books that explain the Japanese way of keeping things **tidy**. The important point common to both of these is that people overseas are aware of the words and actions, even though the Japanese did not **intend** this to happen.

Every culture has two sides on the same coin. If the traditional good qualities of a country's culture are one side of the coin, then the customs and **exclusive practices** that emerge from them are the other side. Japanese culture is no exception. If one **brags** about one's own culture, it will be seen as an act of exclusivity.

Therefore, one man's solitary bow to a golf course was seen as having a **humble** and **silent beauty**, especially because Mr. Hayafuji did not intend it to do so. Even if it is the same action, the appearance of **executives** lining up at a press conference every time a scandal occurs and bowing in the same way before apologizing has been questioned by people overseas as an inexplicable act that is a mere formality and is **without sincerity**.

価値観を海外の人にいかにポジティブに**伝えて**ゆけばよいのかを、今改めて考えてみたくなりました。確かに、アイコンタクトが弱く、ジェスチャーも**控えめ**で、英語力に問題があることも手伝って**寡黙**になりがちな日本人は、世界の中でも最もコミュニケーションが難しい人々だと言われてきました。

その反面、国連でものを大切にする日本人の文化を象徴する「もったいない（MOTTAINAI）」という言葉が披露されたり、日本人ならではの**整理整頓**の方法を解説した書籍がベストセラーになったりと、日本人の価値観が好感をもって受け入れられてきた経緯も無視できません。そのどちらにも共通している大切なポイントは、日本人が**意図**していないにもかかわらず、海外の人がその言葉や行為に気付いていることです。

どのような文化にもコインの表と裏があります。その国の文化の伝統的な良さをコインの表とすれば、そこから生まれる因習や**排他的な行為**は同じコインの裏となります。日本の文化も例外ではありません。自らが自分の文化を**自慢**すれば、それは排他的な行為と捉えられてしまうでしょう。

ですから、ゴルフ場で一人コースに向かって一礼する様子は、早藤さんが意図していなかったからこそ、**謙虚で物言わぬ美しさ**と捉えられたのです。同じ一礼でも、不祥事のたびに記者会見の場で**幹部**が揃って並び、同じように一礼してお詫びをする姿は、型だけにとらわれた**誠意のない**不可解な行為として海外の人から訝しがられます。

▶ケニアの女性環境保護活動家ワンガリ・マータイ氏が、2005年に来日した際「もったいない」という言葉を知って感銘を受け、環境問題を考える重要な概念として同年より「MOTTAINAI」キャンペーンを展開した。

第5章

Thus, a single misstep often results in misunderstandings that do not convey the intentions of the Japanese.

Nevertheless, it is a valuable contribution to the world to communicate the other side of the coin, that is, the positive aspects of our culture and values. Perhaps Japanese people should take pride in our own culture and **become more accustomed to** expressing it openly to others. Whether we can look at our own culture and convey its essential aspects with proper actions is an issue that all Japanese must consider from now on. However, we must also understand that there are ways of communicating that are **appropriate** to the thoughts and values of the other person.

Often, when we watch programs promoting traditional Japanese arts and crafts, we feel conflicted or uncomfortable, as if the programs are daring to boast about the arts and crafts' greatness. In other words, we do not understand why Japanese values of "**modesty**" and "**taciturn**" effort, which are considered virtues, should be promoted and **flaunted**. It is unfortunately true that many foreign intellectuals have pointed this out.

Instead, why don't we pay more attention to the beauty of the little acts that we see in our daily activities? If we remember the "Japanese spirit" that lies beyond such acts, and if we **ponder** their meaning, we will find something that must be handed down from one generation to the next as the other side of the coin.

► modesty ➜ p.218

このように一歩間違えば、日本人の意図が伝わらず誤解の原因となることもよくあるのです。

とはいえ、コインの表側、つまり文化や価値観の良い部分をしっかりと伝え合うことは、世界に向けた貴重な貢献であるとも言えましょう。日本人が自らの文化へのプライドを持ち、それを率直に相手に向けて表現することに**もっと慣れる**べきなのかもしれません。自身の文化を見つめ、その本質的なところをちゃんとした行動と共に伝えられるかは、日本人の誰もがこれから考えなければならない課題なのです。ただ、その伝え方を考えたとき、相手の思考や価値観に**見合った**伝え方があることも理解しなければなりません。

よく、日本の伝統芸能や工芸などをプロモーションする番組を見るとき、そのすごさをあえて自慢しているかのような矛盾や不快を覚えることがあります。つまり、「謙虚」で「寡黙」な努力を美徳とする日本の価値を、なぜアピールし、**ひけらかさ**なければならないのか、わからなくなるからです。このことを指摘する海外の識者が多いことも、残念ながら事実です。

そうではなく、日々の営みの中に見えるちょっとした行為の素晴らしさにもっと注目してみてはどうでしょうか。そんな行為の向こう側にある、「日本人の心」を我々は思い出し、その意味するところを**じっと考えて**みるならば、そこにコインの表として、世代を超えて伝えてゆかなければならない何かを見つけることができるはずです。

第5章

217

Key word

MODESTY 謙遜、慎み深さ

「自分自身や自分の能力について誇りに思ったり、自信を持ちすぎたりしないこと」を指す名詞です。また「〔言動や服装が〕控えめであること」も表します。本文では他にhumble（謙虚な）という形容詞で同様の性質を表しています。対義語としては「尊大（arrogance）」や「高慢（pride）」などが挙げられます。

本文では「謙遜」が美徳とされる日本人の価値観や、さまざまな文化や価値観には良い部分と悪い部分の二面があるということを述べています。そして、自らの文化への誇りをひけらかすことなく「謙虚に」表現していきたいものです。

....

例文

Modesty is a virtue Japanese should value.
謙虚さは日本人が大切にすべき美徳だ。

The modesty that never becomes arrogant is worthy of respect.
決して傲慢にならない謙虚さは尊敬に値する。

A humble leader will attract allies.
謙虚な指導者に人は集まる。

? あなたはどう答える？

What are the aspects of Japanese culture and values you would like to convey?
あなたが伝えていきたい日本人の文化や価値観は何ですか？

ヒント 「場」に敬意を払い競技場を清掃する文化、相手に「礼」を尽くすべくガッツポーズで失格になる剣道や空手など、実例を思い浮かべてその背景にある価値観を伝えましょう。

覚えておくと便利な単語、表現

□ be disqualified for　〜で失格になる

□ be polite and respectful to　（人）に礼を尽くす

□ have a respectful attitude to　〜に敬意を払う

第24話
世界にとって新鮮な
「受け入れる」という発想

Article 24
A Fresh Idea of "Acceptance" for the World

The lesson is to accept the changes. From that acceptance comes a sense of being part of nature, which is actually more of our human nature than trying each day to be happy. After all, why be happy when there is so much work to do?

—— Scott Haas

（変化を受け入れるという発想を学ぶこと。それは、我々が日々お互いの幸福を追求するなかで、より自然な人間のあり方ではないだろうか。そうすれば、幸福を追求するときに四苦八苦する必要もなくなるのではないか、と思うのだが）

A friend of mine is a clinical psychologist named Scott Haas.

He published a book in the US called *Why Be Happy?* The book has had an unexpectedly strong response and has now been translated in 11 countries around the world. The theme of the book is "**Reflections** on the Japanese."

In the 1980s and early 1990s, many books were published that discussed Japan **riding the momentum** of its booming economy. To Westerners, Japan at that time seemed to be just like China today.

Japan's economic revival after overcoming defeat was both surprising and mysterious to Western eyes. From their perspective, Japanese business culture was the exact opposite of theirs, with **individualism**, equality, and freedom as fundamental values. They looked at us as a pyramid-shaped group, an economic army advancing around the world under the motto of "**selflessness and dedication.**"

Just as Western society now feels threatened by China's handling of human rights issues and its seemingly **aggressive** economic expansion, Japan's aggressive global expansion, backed by its economic power at the time, must have seemed like a challenge to Western values themselves.

Therefore, when Japan's economic miracle ended and the country's shadow faded, it was with a **sense of relief** that Western society immediately lost interest in Japan.

Over the next 30 years, Japan came to be accepted not as a threat but as a country **representing** an interesting cultural sphere in a wide range of fields, such as animation and traditional crafts. At the same time, Japanese technology and products,

　私の友人にスコット・ハースという臨床心理学者がい
ます。

　彼は『Why Be Happy?』という一冊の書籍をアメリ
カで出版しました。この書籍が思わぬ反響を呼んで、今
では世界11か国で翻訳されているのです。テーマは「日
本人についての**考察**」です。

　1980年代から90年代初頭にかけて、バブル経済の**勢
いに乗る**日本について考察した書籍が多く出版されまし
た。欧米の人には当時の日本が、ちょうど今の中国のよ
うに映っていたようです。

　敗戦を克服して、経済的な大復興を遂げた日本は、欧
米の目から見れば驚きであり、同時に不可思議な存在で
した。**個人主義**、平等、そして自由を価値観の基本に置
く彼らから見た日本のビジネス文化は、その真逆でした。
ピラミッド型の集団で「**滅私奉公**」をモットーに、世界
に進出してくる経済軍団のように見えたのです。

　今、中国の人権問題への対応、そして**強引**とすら思え
る経済進出の刃に、欧米社会が脅威を感じているように、
当時の日本の経済力にものを言わせたアグレッシブな世
界進出は、欧米の価値観そのものに対する挑戦のように
思えたのでしょう。

　したがって、バブル経済が弾けて日本の影が薄くなっ
たとき、欧米社会は**安堵**と共に、一気に日本から立ち去
ってゆきました。

　その後の30年、日本は脅威ではなく、一つの興味深い
文化圏を**代表する**国として、アニメや伝統工芸などの広
い分野で受け入れられるようになったのです。同時に、自
動車などに代表される日本の技術や製品も、**ごく日常的**

第5章

such as automobiles, came to be used **on a very daily basis**.

Japan was no longer the object of study as an enemy of Western society, and the Japanese were able to shed the **excessive** pride of the time and gradually come to associate with Western society in a natural way.

Now, a little more than 30 years later, the world is **reeling** from the coronavirus disaster. In no other case, it seems, have the differences between cultures around the world been more on display than in the issue of how to deal with this coronavirus.

In the US, the debate over whether or not to wear masks in the face of respect for individual values has made the division of society even clearer, as people are unable to accept each other. In Europe, too, protests against government regulations have led to demonstrations, and politicians seem to be terrified about how the measures they address them with may affect their own bases of power.

Japan, on the other hand, from the perspective of Western society, seemed to provide a **stark contrast**.

Despite some **resentment** over the government's response and the inflexibility of some organizations in the event of an emergency, almost everyone in Japan wore masks, and most organizations, large and small, accepted and quietly **endured** the **self-restraint,** despite fears that restrictions on social activities would seriously affect their daily business operations.

At that time, Scott Haas's *Why Be Happy?* came to mind. It occurred to me that the Japanese "acceptance" of the behavior he describes may have made it easier for the Japanese to coexist with the coronavirus.

► acceptance → p.228

に愛用されるようになりました。

　日本は欧米社会の敵としての研究対象からは外され、日本人自身も当時の**過剰な**プライドを捨て、少しずつ自然に欧米社会と付き合えるようになってきました。

　それから30年あまりが経った今、世界はコロナ禍に**揺れています**。このコロナウイルスとどう付き合うかという課題ほど、世界各地の文化の違いを見せつけられたケースはないようです。

　アメリカでは、個人の価値観を尊重するなかで、マスクをつけるかつけないかということにまで議論が及び、お互いがお互いを受け入れられないことで、社会の分断がより鮮明になりました。ヨーロッパでも、政府の規制への反発からデモが起こり、為政者はそのさじ加減が自らの政権基盤にまで影響を与えかねないと、戦々恐々としているようです。

　それに対して、欧米社会から見た日本は**対照的**でした。

　政府の対応や緊急時に柔軟に動かない組織などへの**憤り**はあるものの、日本人はほぼすべての人がマスクを着用し、社会活動の制限が日々のビジネスに深刻な影響を与えることへの不安はあっても、組織の規模の大小を問わず、大方**自粛**を受け入れて静かに**耐えて**ゆきました。

　そのとき、スコット・ハース氏の『Why Be Happy?』が頭をよぎりました。それは、彼の言う日本人の「**受け入れる**」という行動様式が、日本人をコロナとより共存しやすくしたのではないかと思ったからです。

Since the economic miracle ended, considerations of Japanese culture have been forgotten. The reason *Why Be Happy?* was translated worldwide is probably because the Japanese idea of accepting things was a very natural reference for those suffering in a society affected by the coronavirus.

Acceptance is also an important concept when considering **harmony** and **coexistence** with others. However, in Japan, this often leads to negative effects that sometimes become invisible **peer pressure** and **nip** change and challenge **in the bud**. In the corporate world, an organization still takes precedence over the individual, which inhibits social change toward equality in gender and diversity.

On the other hand, the Japanese tradition of acceptance of what has indeed happened may be an extremely important idea for a society to cope collectively in a disaster, such as the coronavirus.

The roots of the Japanese spirit of acceptance are not unrelated to the religious and social views that the Japanese people have developed over their long history. This idea has both strong and weak sides, two sides of the "cultural" coin.

On the other hand, this idea of "acceptance" is also seen by Westerners as a waste of time. In fact, there are many cases of Japanese companies' human resource development overseas **not going well** because they think it is foolish to accept and endure.

This is nothing more than the difference between a culture that **prioritizes** individual ideas and intentions and one that prioritizes group harmony. In order to **reconcile** the powerful aspects of both sets of values and produce more effective synergy, Japanese people should take another look at the strong side

　バブル崩壊以来、日本文化に関する考察は忘れ去られていました。そのなかで、『Why Be Happy?』が世界各地での翻訳につながった背景は、おそらくコロナ社会で苦しむ人々に、日本人のものごとを受け入れるという発想がごく自然と参考になったからではないでしょうか。

　受容することは、人との**和と共存**を考えるときにも大切な概念です。ただ、日本の場合、それが時には目に見えない**同調圧力**となったり、変化やチャレンジの**芽を摘**んでしまったりするマイナスの作用へとつながることも多くあります。企業では今でも組織が個人よりも優先され、ジェンダーや多様性への平等に向けた社会の変化を阻害しています。

　その反面、確かに起こったことを受け入れるという日本人の伝統的な受容力は、コロナなどの災禍においては社会をまとめて対処してゆくために極めて大切な発想かもしれません。

　日本流の受容の精神のルーツは、日本人が長い歴史のなかで培ってきた宗教観や社会観と無縁ではありません。そして、この発想は強い面と弱い面を併せ持つ、まさに「文化」というコインの両面を備えているわけです。

　一方、この「受け入れてゆく」という発想は、欧米人にとっては時間の無駄としか捉えられない一面もあります。実際、受け入れて耐えることは愚かなことだと彼らが思うことから、日本企業の海外での人材育成が**うまくいかない**事例も多くあります。

　それは、個人の発想や意思を**優先させる**文化と、集団の和を優先させる文化の違いに他なりません。双方の価値観の強い面が**融和して**、より有効的な相乗効果が出すためにも、日本人は「受け入れること」の強い面をもう一度見直すこと。それと同時にコインの裏側を注視し、よ

第5章

of "acceptance." At the same time, we need to keep an eye on the other side of the coin and foster a more flexible and change-resistant society and corporate culture.

If we can accept foreign values as well with that flexibility, then Japanese values will be more widely accepted.

り柔軟で変化に強い社会や企業文化を育成する必要があるのではないでしょうか。

　その柔軟な対応で、海外の価値観をも受容できれば、日本人の価値観もより広く受け入れられるようになるはずです。

第5章

Key word

ACCEPTANCE　受容、受け入れ

「現実の状況について、抵抗せずにありのままを受け入れる姿勢」を表します。心理学の用語として「アクセプタンス」とカタカナで使われることもあり、"acquiescence（黙って従うこと）" という概念に近いとされています。他に「〔招待を〕承諾すること」「〔贈られたものを〕受け取ること」「〔組織や学校への〕採用、合格」などの意味もあります。

本文では日本人の「受け入れ」て耐え忍ぶという行動様式に対する考察と、その発想が併せ持つ強い面と弱い面を見直したうえで、より柔軟に海外の価値観も「受容」できることが望ましいと述べているのです。

例文

She expressed acceptance of her suffering.
彼女は苦しみを受け入れることを示した。

I appreciate your acceptance very much.
ご承諾いただき、大変感謝しております。

Acceptance rates for this university are very low.
この大学の合格率は非常に低い。

❓ あなたはどう答える？

Why is "acceptance" possible in Japan?
日本ではなぜ「受け入れる」ことが可能なのでしょうか？

> **ヒント**　非常時でも冷静さを失わない礼儀正しさ・秩序を保つ反面、コロナ禍での「自粛警察」は議論を呼びました。社会の調和・安定を重んじるがゆえの行動にも二面性があります。

覚えておくと便利な単語、表現

☐ **endure hardship**　苦難に耐える

☐ **value social harmony**　社会の調和を重んじる

☐ **vigilante**　自警団、私的制裁を加える人

228

第6章

世界、そして未来への課題

Chapter 6

Challenges for the World and the Future

第25話
格差社会に影響を与える地球温暖化

Article 25
Global Warming Affecting Disparities

The poor are punished: Dorian lays bare inequality in the Bahamas

—— The Guardian

（貧しき者が裁かれる：ドリアンはバハマの不平等を暴き出した）

The Glasgow Climate Accord was adopted in Scotland in November 2021 to **curb** global warming and address climate change. It included a commitment to strive to limit the **rise in global temperatures** to within 1.5°C above the level at the time of the Industrial Revolution, by 2100. At the conference, while developed countries tried to reduce **fossil fuel** use, the agreement on the **abolition** of **coal power generation** was weakened from "abolition" to "**phase-out**" due to opposition from India and China. International alignment is not easy to achieve.

On the other hand, when Russia invaded Ukraine in 2022 and Western European countries and Russia confronted each other, there was growing concern that the supply of natural gas and other resources from Russia would be cut off. This, in turn, will hasten the Western nations' shift away from dependence on conventional resources, such as fossil fuels, and may also accelerate technological innovation to this end.

The most significant concern about global warming is that **rising seawater temperatures** will cause polar ice caps to melt and sea levels to rise, resulting in various climatic changes.

Less than a month after the conference in Glascow ended, Typhoon Rai symbolized such concerns when it landed following the end of the typhoon season in the Philippines on December 16, 2021 and caused extensive damage to the area.

　2021年11月にグラスゴーで、地球温暖化を**抑制し**気候変動に対応するためのグラスゴー気候合意が採択されました。採択には、2100年には産業革命の時点より**地球の気温上昇**を1.5度以内に抑えるよう努力することが盛り込まれています。会議では、**化石燃料**の使用を抑えるために先進国がより踏み込もうとした反面、**石炭発電の廃止**についてはインドや中国の反対によって、その表現が「廃止」から「**段階的に削減**」へと弱められました。国際的な足並みはなかなか揃いません。

　一方で、2022年にロシアがウクライナに侵攻し、西欧諸国とロシアが対立すると、ロシアからの天然ガスなどの資源の供給が断たれる懸念が広がりました。これによって逆に西欧諸国は化石燃料など従来型の資源依存からの脱却を急ぎ、そのための技術革新も加速するかもしれません。

　地球温暖化で最も懸念されるのは、**海水温の上昇**により、極地の氷が解けて海面が上昇することで、様々な気候異変が起こることでしょう。

　グラスゴーでの会議からひと月も経たない2021年12月16日、そんな懸念を象徴するように、台風「ライ（オデット）」が台風シーズンを過ぎたあとにフィリピンに上陸し、現地に甚大な被害を与えました。

第6章

In the US, the hot and dry summer season has been accompanied by a **rash of wildfires** on a scale not seen in the past. Similar fires have also occurred in Australia and other countries.

Indeed, similar disasters have been occurring around the world recently, including Hurricane Dorian, which struck the Bahamas, an island nation off the coast of Florida, three years ago. The Bahamas has a well-established image as a tax haven and warm tourist destination. You must wonder who was affected when you hear that a major hurricane **made landfall** on such an island and left many people dead, injured, or missing.

In reality, the Bahamas is not just an island reserved for the **wealthy**.

It is also home to many poor immigrants from Haiti, another Caribbean Island nation. The Bahamas, like other wealthy countries, has a severe **disparity** problem. A short flight north from the center of the Bahamas takes you to the Abaco Islands. The poor people from Haiti who lived there were **devastated** by Hurricane Dorian.

In other words, global warming caused by **environmental pollution** and wealth disparity are not two separate issues facing humanity.

Recently, it has been in the news that **mercury** has been found in the feathers of penguins in Antarctica due to human-made pollution. The increasing number of **endangered species** of animals and plants, such as polar bears, has long been viewed as a problem. When such environmental pollution **accelerates** global warming, many of the victims will be people suffering from poverty.

The global disparity in wealth is considered a North-South

▶ disparity ➤ p.238

　アメリカでも熱暑と乾燥によって、夏になれば過去には見られなかった大規模な**山火事が頻発**しています。同様の火災はオーストラリアなどでも起こっています。

　確かに最近似たような災害が世界中で起きています。2019年には、ハリケーン「ドリアン」がフロリダの沖合の島国バハマを襲いました。バハマといえば、タックス・ヘイヴンの楽園で、温暖な観光地というイメージが定着しています。そんな島に大型ハリケーンが**上陸**し、多くの死傷者、行方不明者が出たと聞けば、誰が被害に遭ったのかと思うはずです。

　実は、バハマは決して**富裕層**だけが特権を享受している島ではないのです。

　そこにはカリブ海のもう一つの島国ハイチなどからの貧しい移民も多く住んでいます。バハマも他の裕福な国々と同様に、深刻な**格差**の問題を抱えているのです。バハマの中心地から飛行機で北にほんのわずか飛べば、アバコ諸島に到着します。ハリケーン「ドリアン」で壊滅的な**打撃を受けた**のは、そこに住むハイチからの貧しい人々だったのです。

　つまり、**環境汚染**による地球の温暖化と富の格差とは、人類が抱える別々の課題として分離できるものではないのです。

　最近では人類が作り出した汚染によって、南極のペンギンまでもが羽毛から**水銀**が発見されていることが話題になりました。ホッキョクグマに代表される動植物に**絶滅危惧種**が増えていることも長年問題視されています。そうした環境汚染が地球の温暖化に**拍車をかけた**とき、被害を受ける人の多くが貧困に苦しむ人々ということになるのです。

　地球規模で見れば貧富の格差は南北問題とされ、アフ

▶タックス・ヘイヴンは、一定の課税が軽減または免除される国や地域のことで「相税回避地」とも呼ばれる。税制上の優遇措置を域外の企業に対して戦略的に設けることで富裕層や多国籍企業の資金が集まる。

第6章

problem, and the poverty generated in the South, such as in Africa and Latin America, has created a **flow of immigrants** to Europe and North America, becoming a social issue. The problem of Haitian immigrants in the Bahamas has again brought to light the "North-South problem" that **lurks** within such a rich country.

There are currently 850 million hungry people in the world. One in nine human beings is threatened with lack of food. We must also pay attention to the **vicious cycle** in which such problems of hunger and poverty accelerate environmental pollution. For example, more than 2,500 **forest fires** occur each year in the Amazon River Basin of Brazil. This **has repercussions** around the world, as forests that greatly exceed the size of Tokyo are disappearing. The area that will be burned is the northern part of Brazil, an **economically backward** and poverty-prone region. Deforestation is also caused by sometimes deliberate attempts to start fires and expand farmland for the purpose of increasing income in such areas. Here we can see a typical example of how the global environmental problem and the disparity problem are closely intertwined.

The reality that hunger lives side by side with people enjoying cocktails on the beach in the Bahamas is a reality that can be seen in many other parts of the world. As affluence spread throughout the world in the second half of the 20th century, it seemed that the problem of hunger would gradually be resolved. Recently, however, the pace of healing has slowed dramatically, and some reports suggest that we may be **slipping back** to the past. Addressing environmental issues requires overcoming the other challenge of considering these social disparities.

リカや中南米など南側で生まれる貧困が、ヨーロッパや北米への**移民の流れ**を作り出し、それが社会問題となっていると言われています。バハマでのハイチ系移民の問題は、そんな豊かな国の中に**潜む**「南北問題」を改めて浮き彫りにしたのです。

　現在、世界の飢餓人口は8億5000万人とされています。人類の9人に1人が飢餓の恐怖に見舞われているのです。そうした飢餓や貧困の問題が、逆に環境汚染を加速させるという**悪循環**についても、我々は配慮しなければならないのです。例えば、ブラジルのアマゾン川流域で、**森林火災**が毎年2500件以上発生し、東京都の面積を大きく超える森林が消失している現実は、世界に**波紋を広げて**います。森林が焼失する地域はブラジルの北部で、**経済的に立ち遅れ**、貧困が問題となっている地域です。そんな地域の所得を向上させる目的で森林を伐採し、時には意図的に火災を起こし、農地を広げようとしていることが森林破壊の原因でもあるのです。地球の環境問題と格差問題が密接に絡み合っている典型的な実例がここに見えてきます。

　バハマのビーチでカクテルを楽しむ人々のすぐそばに飢餓が同居している実態は、世界各地にも見られる現実です。20世紀後半になって、豊かさが世界に浸透し、徐々に飢餓の問題が解決に向かうのではないかと思われていました。しかし、最近その治癒のペースが失速し、過去へ**逆戻り**しつつあるという報道もあるのです。環境問題に取り組むには、こうした社会の格差への配慮というもう一つの課題の克服が必要なのです。

Key word

DISPARITY　格差、不均衡

　本文では「貧富の格差（wealth disparity）」について述べていますが、残念なことに世界にはこの他にもさまざまな格差が存在します。健康と医療の質における「健康格差（health disparity）」や教育の機会や質に生じる「教育格差（educational disparity）」、選挙における一票の価値が異なる「一票の格差（disparity in vote values）」などです。こうした格差を「是正する」ことを表すときは、redress（正す）／reduce（縮小する）／adjust（調節する）などの動詞を使うことができます。格差があるという事実を他人事ではなく自分事として受け止め、自分にできることは何か、私たち一人ひとりが考え行動していきたいものです。

例文

Economic disparities in Japan are widening.
日本では経済格差が拡大している。

Opinions are divided on whether the disparity in vote values violates the Constitution.
一票の格差が憲法に違反するかどうかは、意見が分かれるところだ。

The first step in redressing disparities in gender is to identify the fact that disparities exist in our society.
ジェンダー格差を是正する第一歩は、まず社会に格差が存在する事実を明らかにすることです。

 あなたはどう答える？

What is Japan's approach to global warming?
日本の地球温暖化に対する取り組みはどのようなものでしょうか？

ヒント　政府目標は温室効果ガスを2030年度までに2013年度比で46％に削減、2050年までに排出ゼロです。新築住宅・建築物の省エネ規制や自動車の脱炭素化などに取り組んでいます。

覚えておくと便利な単語、表現

☐ **emission of greenhouse gases**　温室効果ガスの排出
☐ **ensure a stable energy supply**　エネルギーの安定供給を確保する
☐ **numerical target**　数値目標

第26話
南北問題と民主主義の確執に揺れる
ノーベル賞

Article 26
Nobel Prize Shaken by North-South Problem and Democracy Feuds

Philippine court allows Maria Ressa to attend Nobel Peace Prize ceremony after days of growing international pressure on the government.

—— New York Times

（このところ国際的に広がりを見せた政府への圧力に、フィリピンの裁判所は、マリア・レッサ氏がノーベル平和賞の授賞式に参加することを許可）

The 2021 Nobel Peace Prize was awarded to Filipino journalist Maria Ressa and Russian journalist Dmitry Muratov. Both were recognized for their various activities in pursuing **freedom of the press**.

One of them, Maria Ressa was born in the Philippines and later immigrated to the US. After studying theater along with molecular biology at Princeton University, she majored in journalism at the University of the Philippines and later worked as a journalist, including time as CNN's Manila Bureau Chief. In 2012, she helped found Rappler, the Philippines' first online news site, and served as its CEO.

She **became prominent** when she criticized President Duterte for his strong-arm tactics to combat drugs and **bribery**. She attacked him for **violating human rights** by shooting suspects to death, **incarcerating** them in unforgiving and unsanitary detention centers, and intimidating opposing politicians to fight bribery. At that time, Rappler was **ordered to suspend its activities** on the grounds that the US capital was manipulating it, and Maria Ressa was arrested on **defamation charges**. However, she continued to protest against the suppression of the press, leading to her winning the Nobel Peace Prize.

However, the stereotyping of the Duterte administration as the villain and Maria Ressa as the "friend of justice" is questionable. In the background of this award, the complex reality of the North-South problem, which cannot be measured by the **scale of developed countries**, seems to have been drowned out.

Of course, freedom of the press is an extremely important right. Not being able to criticize the war on Ukraine, as is the case in Russia, is a major problem. And journalism is also essential as

　2021年のノーベル平和賞は、フィリピンのジャーナリストであるマリア・レッサ氏と、ロシアのジャーナリスト、ドミトリー・ムラトフ氏の2名に贈られました。2名とも**報道の自由**を求めた様々な活動が評価されたのです。

　このうち、マリア・レッサ氏はフィリピンで生まれ、その後アメリカに移住。プリンストン大学で分子生物学と共に演劇を学んだ後、フィリピン大学でジャーナリズムを専攻し、その後ジャーナリストとしてCNNマニラ支局長などを歴任しました。そして、2012年にはフィリピン初のオンライン・ニュースサイト「ラップラー」の創設に関わり、同社のCEOを務めたのです。

ノーベル平和賞の授賞式が
行われるノルウェーの首都
オスロ

　彼女が**注目された**のは、彼女が麻薬や**賄賂**を撲滅するために強権を発動していたドゥテルテ大統領を批判したときでした。被疑者を射殺したり、容赦なく不衛生な拘置所に**収監**したり、対立する政治家を賄賂撲滅のために威嚇したことなどに対して、**人権の蹂躙**であると批判したのです。そんなとき、ラップラーが米国資本に操られているとして**活動停止を命じられ**、マリア・レッサ氏も**名誉毀損容疑**で逮捕されます。しかし彼女が、そうした報道の抑圧に屈せず抗議を続けたことが、ノーベル平和賞の受賞につながったのです。

ロドリゴ・ドゥテルテ

　ただ、ドゥテルテ政権を悪役とし、マリア・レッサ氏を「正義の味方」にするステレオタイプ化には疑問が残ります。この受賞の背景では、**先進国の尺度では測れ**ない南北問題の複雑な現実が、かき消されているように思えます。

　もちろん、報道の自由は極めて大切な権利です。今のロシアのようにウクライナへの戦争を批判できなくなることは大きな問題です。そして、ジャーナリズムは、政

第6章

a check on politics and power. But to simply criticize President Duterte's **strong-arm politics** while covering up the depth of the social problems in the Philippines, for example, would give the world an unintended misunderstanding.

The drug problem in the Philippines was serious. Many people have lost their lives in drug-related conflicts, and those who tried to eradicate them have been the target of assassinations and **kidnappings**. Furthermore, bribery has been rampant, and the **impartial administration** of government has been hindered. President Duterte openly challenged this problem and exercised his authority.

Indeed, it is possible to criticize his policies, which have relentlessly introduced **police power** to eliminate social unrest, as populism with no regard for human rights. However, it is questionable whether the media has given as much coverage to how frightened Filipino citizens were by a society tainted by drugs and bribes.

Filipinos are always afraid of getting sick. That is because a minor illness can lead to **life-threatening problems**. In particular, **low-income earners** are constantly facing **life-or-death fears**. The reason medical facilities are not sufficient is that even public hospital building projects have been entwined with bribery and **political corruption**.

Speaking of public works, riverbank protection works have been also poorly done for the same reason, and floods still engulf the area during the rainy season in one local city. Every time a typhoon hits, citizens evacuate to the second floor, and flooding above ground level is a daily occurrence. Of course, **hygiene** will also be affected. The list of such examples is endless.

As a result, the Philippines' economic development has

治や権力へのチェック機能としても必要不可欠です。し
かし、例えば、フィリピンでの社会問題の根深さにふた
をして、ただドゥテルテ大統領の**強権政治**を批判するこ
とは、思わぬ誤解を世界に与えてしまいます。

　フィリピンのドラッグ問題は深刻でした。麻薬に関わ
る抗争などで命を落とす人も多く、撲滅活動をすれば暗
殺や**誘拐**の標的にもされました。しかも、賄賂が横行し、
公正な行政活動が阻害されてきました。この問題に公然
と挑み、強権を振るったのがドゥテルテ大統領です。

　確かに、社会不安の除去に**警察権力**を容赦なく導入し
た彼の政策を、人権を無視したポピュリズムだと批判す
ることは可能です。しかし、フィリピンの市民が麻薬と
賄賂に汚染された社会に怯えていた様子を、メディアが
同じ規模で海外に報道してきたかというと、疑問が残り
ます。

　フィリピンの人々は常に病気にかかることを恐れてい
ます。それは、ささいな病気が**命の問題**につながるから
です。特に、**低所得者**は常に**生死の恐怖**と隣り合わせで
す。なぜ医療施設が充実していないかといえば、病院を
建てるという公共の事業にまで賄賂がからみ、**政治の腐
敗**が影響を与えてきたからです。

　公共工事といえば、ある地方都市では、同様の理由で
川の護岸工事も手順が悪く、いまだに雨季には洪水が街
を飲み込みます。台風のたびに市民は2階に避難し、床上
浸水は日常のできごとです。当然、**衛生面**にも影響が出
てきます。こうした事例を挙げればきりがありません。

　その結果、人口や国土の大きさ、高い英語の**普及率**と

第6章

been overshadowed despite its population, land size, and high English-language **penetration rate**. This is not unrelated to the fact that the Philippines had long been a colony of powerful nations. Moreover, until recently, the US supported a bribe-ridden regime, partly for military purposes during the Cold War. It is difficult to overcome these **negative legacies**, nurture the **people's will**, and develop the country.

Maria Ressa is undoubtedly an excellent and courageous journalist. But she was educated in the US, a country far more affluent than the Philippines, and she confronted President Duterte with the **democratic ideals** of that country. The American public cheered her on, and that became a milestone on the way to the Nobel Prize.

Of course, the Philippine government's response to Maria Ressa is questionable. On the other hand, however, what should be emphasized here is that the gap in consciousness between her and the general Filipino public is symbolic of the North-South problem and the global **disparity issue**.

Each region of the world has its own **shackles** due to its long history. If we ignore them and criticize others too much with Western-style democratic ideals, it will be misunderstood as prejudice from the West. A typical example of this was the rise of the Taliban in Afghanistan in 2021, which shocked the world. The **imposition** of values can impede the path to democratization and lead people to the opposite of what is expected.

► imposition → p.246

いう背景がありながら、フィリピンの経済発展にも影を落としたのです。これは、フィリピンが長い間、列強の植民地であったことと無縁ではありません。しかも、最近までアメリカは賄賂にまみれた政権を、冷戦下での軍事的な目的もあり支持してきました。こうした**負の遺産**を克服し、**民意**を育て、国を発展させることは困難です。

　マリア・レッサ氏は、確かに優秀で勇気あるジャーナリストです。しかし彼女はフィリピンとは比べものにならない豊かな国アメリカで教育を受け、そこでの**民主主義の理想**をもって、ドゥテルテ大統領と対峙しました。そんな彼女にアメリカの民意が声援を送り、ノーベル賞へのマイルストーンとなりました。

　もちろん、マリア・レッサ氏へのフィリピン政府の対応には疑問が残ります。しかし一方で、彼女とフィリピンの一般民衆との意識のギャップこそが、南北問題や世界の**格差問題**を象徴していることを、ここで押さえておきたいのです。

　世界各地にそれぞれの長い歴史による**足かせや手かせ**があります。それを無視して、単に欧米流の民主主義の理想をもって相手を批判しすぎると、それは欧米からの偏見と誤解されます。その典型的な例が、2021年世界に衝撃を与えたアフガニスタンでのタリバンの台頭でした。価値観の**押しつけ**は逆に民主化への道筋を妨げ、その結果、期待とはまったく逆の結果へと人々を導いてしまうこともあるのです。

第6章

Key word

IMPOSITION 押し付け、強制

　「仕事や義務、税金などを課すこと」あるいは「課せられた負担」そのものを指します。または「騙すこと、詐欺」の意味もあります。動詞形はimpose（押し付ける、課す）です。

　本文ではimposition of values（価値観の押し付け）とでてきますが、社会不安の大きいフィリピンの現状を考慮せず、強権政治を発動するドゥテルテ政権に対して、一方的に「民主主義」や「正義」を押し付けて批判することの危うさを指摘しているのです。価値観や尺度は国や地域、社会、人によってもそれぞれです。

例文

The imposition of values only creates a backlash from people.
価値観の押し付けは人々の反発を生むだけだ。

The heavy imposition of tax might dampen the desire to work.
重い課税によって働く意欲が削がれるかもしれない。

Schools should not impose religious teaching.
学校は宗教的な教えを押し付けてはならない。

? あなたはどう答える？

Is freedom of the press protected in Japan?
日本では報道の自由は守られているのですか？

ヒント　「国境なき記者団」報道の自由度ランキング2022で日本は71位と、G7の中では最下位です。大企業の情報をメディアが自主的に控える、政府からの圧力などがその理由です。

覚えておくと便利な単語、表現

☐ major company　大企業
☐ prompt a form of self-censorship　自己検閲を促す
☐ under pressure from the government　政府からの圧力を受けて

第27話
政治とスポーツ、そして芸術との関係とは

Article 27
What Is the Relationship between Politics, Sports, and the Arts?

Dina Asher-Smith has backed the relaxation of rules around athlete protests at the Tokyo Olympics, calling protest "a fundamental human right"

—— BBC

（ディナ・アッシャー＝スミス選手が、東京オリンピックでの「基本的な人権」への抗議についてのルールを緩和すべきだとする選手の抗議をサポート）

British track and field athlete Dina Asher-Smith made headlines when she argued at the Tokyo Olympics in 2021 that the rules about athletes protesting for fundamental **human rights** should be **relaxed**.

She formally **challenged** the IOC's ban on political protests at the Olympics, saying it is a human right to **express one's political will**.

There is a slogan: "Sports and music transcend national borders to bring peace."

But the reality is that sports and the arts have always been used and exploited by those fighting for their rights and those in power trying to protect the **prestige** of the state. As long as there are various political issues in the world, neither artists nor athletes should be able to avoid this.

Here is one example.

Exactly 191 years before Dina Asher-Smith protested (1830), the July Revolution took place in France, toppling once again the French dynasty that had been in power since the **downfall** of Napoleon. At that time, Chopin, who was attracting attention as a musician, was deeply saddened by the fact that his **native** Poland was being overwhelmed by Russia. It is said that Chopin hoped that France, which the July Revolution had democratized, would send support to the **civil uprising** in Poland in November of that year but was very disappointed when it did not happen.

Soon after that, in 1831, Chopin presented his "Revolutionary Étude" in Vienna, a work filled with his feelings. Chopin then began his career in France, where he continued to publish music with Polish motifs for the rest of his life. Understanding that his

▶ right → p.254

　イギリスの陸上選手ディナ・アッシャー＝スミス氏が、オリンピックで選手が基本的な**人権**を守るための抗議をすることに関するルールを**緩和**すべきだと、2021年の東京オリンピックで主張したことが話題になりました。

　政治的な意思表明をすることは人間の権利だとして、IOCがオリンピックでの政治的な抗議活動を禁止していることに対して、正式に**異議を申し立て**たのです。

　スポーツと音楽は国境を超えて平和を、というスローガンがあります。

　しかし、権利を求めて戦う人にも、国家の**威信**を守ろうとする権力者にも、スポーツと芸術は常に活用され、利用されてきた現実があるのです。実際に世界で様々な政治問題がある以上、芸術家もスポーツ選手も、これを避けて通ることはできないはずです。

　一つの事例を挙げてみましょう。

　ディナ・アッシャー＝スミス選手が抗議を行ったちょうど191年前(1830年)に、フランスで7月革命が起こり、ナポレオンの**失脚**以来続いていたフランスの王朝が再び打倒されました。その当時、音楽家として注目を集めていたショパンは、**祖国ポーランド**がロシアに席巻されていることに心を痛めていました。その年の11月にポーランドで起きた**市民の蜂起**に、ショパンは7月革命で民主化されたフランスが支援を送るのではと期待したものの、それがなかったことにひどく失望したと伝えられています。

　それから間もなく、1831年に彼がウィーンで発表した「革命のエチュード」は、そうした彼の思いが詰め込まれた作品です。その後、フランスで活動を始めたショパンは、終生ポーランドをモチーフにした作品を発表し続け

フレデリック・ショパン

第6章

beautiful melodies were born from his anger and sadness over the situation at that time in his homeland is a significant clue to understanding Chopin's music.

This episode symbolizes how important it is for artists and athletes to have a firm political stance and a sense of citizenship.

Once, for example, at the Mexico Olympics in 1968, black American athletes Tommie Smith and John Carlos wore black gloves and raised their arms on the podium to **protest racial discrimination** in the US. This sparked worldwide concern about **black racism** and led to the expansion of the **civil rights movement** in the US. The acts of Chopin, Tommie Smith and John Carlos, or Dina Asher can be considered courageous.

Whether it was the recent Tokyo Olympics or the winter Beijing Paralympics, the world situation changed rapidly during the period of the event, and the world's major media outlets also devoted time to reporting on them, so the impact of Olympic coverage was relatively small. The Paralympics coverage in China was **significantly reduced** due to Russia's invasion of Ukraine. During the Tokyo Olympics, media attention was also focused on the **precarious** situation in Afghanistan due to the withdrawal of US troops from the country.

There was also significant news coverage of a **bipartisan** group of US legislators who launched an effort to get China to reconsider hosting the Winter Olympics in China, where the

ます。彼の美しい旋律は、彼の祖国の置かれている現状への怒りと悲しみから生まれていることを理解することが、ショパンを知る大きなヒントとなります。

このエピソードは、芸術家やスポーツ選手がしっかりとした政治的なスタンス、一市民としての意識を持つことがいかに大切かということを象徴しています。

以前は、例えば1968年のメキシコシティオリンピックで、アメリカの黒人選手トミー・スミス氏とジョン・カーロス氏が、アメリカでの**人種差別**に**抗議**して、黒い手袋をはめた拳を掲げて表彰式に臨んだことがありました。このことで、**黒人差別**への関心が世界に広がり、アメリカでの**公民権運動**の拡大にもつながりました。ショパンやトミー・スミスとジョン・カーロス、あるいはディナ・アッシャー＝スミスの行為は勇気あるものと言えましょう。

直近の東京オリンピックにせよ、冬の北京パラリンピックにせよ、開催期間中に世界情勢が目まぐるしく動いたことで、世界の主要メディアはそちらの報道にも時間を割くため、相対的にオリンピック報道のインパクトが希薄になりました。実際、中国でのパラリンピックはロシアのウクライナ侵攻のために、報道自体が**大幅に縮小され**てしまいました。東京オリンピックのときも、アメリカが軍隊をアフガニスタンから撤収したことでアフガン情勢が極めて**不安定**になり、メディアの注目が集まりました。

また、**少数民族**の人権が守られていない中国での冬季オリンピックの開催を再考するように、アメリカの**超党派議員**が活動を開始したというニュースも大きく報道さ

1968年メキシコシティオリンピック男子200m走の表彰台で、拳を掲げる金メダリストのトミー・スミス（中央）と銅メダリストのジョン・カーロス（右）

第6章

251

human rights of **ethnic minorities** are not being protected.

Since these complex global issues are also occurring in the countries where the athletes participating in the Olympics and Paralympics are from, it can be said that the issues of sports and politics are **inseparable.**

At the opening ceremony of the Tokyo Olympics, a **moment of silence was observed** for the athletes who lost their lives in the attack on Israeli athletes in Munich in 1972. There was also speculation that while showing respect for the silent prayers for the athletes who lost their lives in terrorist acts at the time, the Japanese government's intention was also to **dodge** the criticism that the Japanese Olympic Committee has received for remarks that **discriminate against women.** Major countries worldwide are also clearly using the Olympics for political purposes to promote their **agendas**, national prestige, and internal political stability.

And yet, from Chopin to Dina Asher-Smith, the expression of will by artists and individual athletes has always been highly restricted.

We should look at the Olympic Games and their politics, taking these themes more seriously so that this world celebration will not be used for mere political populism.

れていました。

　こうした世界の複雑な問題は、オリンピックやパラリンピックに参加している選手の出身国でも起きているわけですから、確かにスポーツと政治の問題は**切っても切り離せない**課題であると言えるはずです。

　東京オリンピックの開会式では、1972年のミュンヘン大会で起きた、イスラエル選手襲撃事件で命を落とした選手への**黙祷が行われました**。当時のテロ行為で命を落とした選手への黙祷には敬意を表しながらも、日本のオリンピック委員会が**女性差別**発言などで批判を受けてきたことを**かわす**日本政府の意図がそこにあったのでは、という憶測も飛び交いました。そして、世界の主要国も、あきらかにオリンピックを政治的に利用し、自国の**スタンス**や国威、そして内政の安定のための特効薬へとつなげています。

▶1972年9月5日に西ドイツのミュンヘンでパレスチナ武装組織「黒い九月」により実行されたテロ事件。オリンピックの選手村に侵入した組織メンバーによってイスラエルのアスリート11名が亡くなった。

　それでありながら、ショパンからディナ・アッシャー＝スミスへとつながる芸術家や個々のスポーツ選手の意思表示には、常に強い制限がかけられているのです。

　オリンピックと政治の課題を通して、この世界の祭典が単なる政治的なポピュリズムに利用されないためにも、こうしたテーマを我々はもっと真剣に考えるべきなのです。

第6章

Key word

RIGHT 〔法律・伝統に基づく〕権利

　英語でニュースを読むときは、この「権利」という言葉がどのような権利を指すのか、さまざまな熟語で理解しておく必要があります。本文では、スポーツ選手が政治的な意思表明をすることはhuman rights、すなわち「人権」だというある選手の主張について書かれています。人権とは人間が生まれながらにもち、国家権力によっても侵されない普遍的権利です。また、同じく本文にでてきた「公民権」はcivil rightsといいます。19世紀後半には白人による人種差別が合法とされていたアメリカで、その差別撤廃を求めた公民権運動がおこり、法の上での平等を勝ち取りました。しかし、21世紀の現在も人種や民族間での差別行為や差別感情は根深く残っているのです。

例文

Is it not a granted right for athletes to express their political will on the playing field?
スポーツ選手が競技の場で政治的な意思を表明することは、認められた権利ではないのだろうか？

Human rights are fundamental rights that people are born with.
人権とは、人間が生まれながらにしてもっている基本的な権利だ。

During the 1950s and 1960s, blacks in the United States engaged in a popular social movement called the Civil Rights Movement.
1950年代から60年代にかけて、アメリカ合衆国の黒人たちが公民権運動と呼ばれる大衆的な社会運動を展開した。

 あなたはどう答える？

Do Japanese athletes not express their will?
日本のスポーツ選手が意思表明をすることはないのですか？

ヒント テニスの大坂なおみ選手が2020年に人種差別に抗議し試合を棄権した際、スポーツと政治を混同させるなという反応が寄せられました。この一件、あなたはどう考えますか？

覚えておくと便利な単語、表現

☐ **human rights issue** 　人権の問題
☐ **keep politics separate from sports** 　政治とスポーツを切り離す
☐ **withdraw from the match** 　試合を棄権する

第28話
文明の磁場の逆転が進む中で
迷走するアジアとアメリカ

Article 28
Asia and America Lost in the Progressive Reversal
of Civilization's Magnetic Field

Do the current contradictions in the economy and society represent the birth pains of a new society for the future? Time will tell.
——『日英対訳 日本の歴史』（IBCパブリッシング刊）

（現在の経済、そして社会の矛盾は新しい未来を生み出すための陣痛なのか？ それはその時代の中にいる限り、我々にはわからない）

It is well known that **reversals of the magnetic field** have occurred frequently since the birth of the earth: the positions of
the N and S poles are swapped. Let's put this phenomenon in
the context of the history of human **values**. Do humans not have
reversals of the magnetic field of civilization?

To answer this question, we turn to Silicon Valley. The region
represented by Silicon Valley is a stronghold of American liberal
forces. Many American liberals originally grew up in a **Christian
society**, and then **broke away from** that tradition and carved out
their own careers with new values. The trigger was the change in
American society after the Vietnam War.

After the Vietnam War, the US population of Indian, Chinese,
Vietnamese, and Korean immigrants **grew rapidly**, and Asian
culture was injected into the country, especially on the East and
West coasts.

During the 80s and 90s, this new cultural phenomenon
was **embraced** by people trying to break away from traditional
American values. They were influenced by Asian culture but
maintained the Christian **guilt** and morals on which they were
based. They gradually mixed old and new values. On top of
that, they incorporated Asian values as a symbol of **diversity**.
Moreover, in the process, a strong sense of guilt for discrimination and prejudice was fostered. In addition, their **skepticism** of
capitalism dominated by conventional industry led them to be
sensitive to issues facing the entire planet, such as protecting animals and forest resources, and concerns about global warming.

Meanwhile, computer science has grown into an industry, and
biotechnology has advanced dramatically in the US, supported

► value → p.262

　磁場の逆転が地球の誕生以来、頻繁に起こっていることはよく知られています。N極とS極との位置が入れ替わるのです。この現象を人類の**価値観**の歴史に照らしてみましょう。人間には文明という磁場の逆転現象がないのかと。

　そのために、シリコンバレーに目を向けます。シリコンバレーに代表される地域は、アメリカのリベラル勢力の拠点です。アメリカのリベラル層の多くは、元々**キリスト教社会**に育ち、その後そうした伝統と**訣別**し、新しい価値観の中で自分たちのキャリアを切り開いてきました。きっかけはベトナム戦争以後のアメリカ社会の変化でした。

　ベトナム戦争の後、アメリカにはインドや中国、ベトナムや韓国系移民などの人口が**急増**し、アジアの文化がアメリカの東西両海岸を中心に注入されました。

　80年代から90年代にかけて、そんな新しい文化現象が、従来のアメリカの価値観から脱皮しようとした人々に**受容された**のです。彼らは、アジア文化の影響を受けながら、そのベースにあったキリスト教の**罪悪感**やモラルは維持していました。新旧の価値観をミックスさせていったのです。その上で、アジアの価値観を**多様性**の象徴として取り入れたのです。さらに、その過程で、差別や偏見への徹底した罪悪感が育まれました。また、従来型の産業に支配された資本主義への**懐疑**から、動物や森林資源の保護、温暖化への懸念など、地球全体が直面する課題に敏感に対応するようになったのです。

　一方で、アメリカではこうした人々や優秀な移民に支えられてコンピュータサイエンスが産業として成長し、

▶1954年に始まったベトナム戦争はテレビ放送が普及してから最初に勃発した大規模な戦争で、悲惨な実態を目の当たりにした若者を中心に反戦運動が拡がり、そこから既成文化への反発とカウンターカルチャーに結びついた。

第6章

by these people and other talented immigrants. Although there are concerns about whether humans will be able to handle developments such as AI, many believe that they will bring about new upgrades that raise the quality of industry.

What about Asia, then, which has influenced the US? Take Japan, for example. After World War II, Japan **thoroughly** adopted Western democratic systems and worked to **revitalize** its industries. However, introducing only **external** systems and mechanisms while putting aside the values that supported such systems caused "**indigestion**" in Japanese society afterward.

In China, on the other hand, a **communist regime** came to power after years of social turmoil. After experiencing the Cultural Revolution, the country **made compromises with** capitalism and achieved a remarkable increase in GDP. However, these processes seem to have left a common negative legacy in many Asian countries. In prioritizing the development of their industries, the positive aspects of the various values that initially existed in Asia have been **abandoned**.

For example, Japan prioritized education for industrial development, and the **pursuit of humanity**, the most basic part of education, was **put on the back burner**. People who were obedient to the organization were considered superior. As a result, values such as "flexibility," "humility," and "harmony," which had existed in traditional Japanese society, became **diluted**.

Of course, there are negative aspects to these traditional values. However, even the positive aspects were nearly destroyed when the negative aspects were removed.

In China, **Confucian morality**, the core of Asian values, collapsed through the Cultural Revolution, followed by moral hazards caused by **money worship**. Furthermore, a **controlled**

バイオテクノロジーも格段に進歩しました。AIなどの発達を人類が消化できるのかという危惧はあるものの、多くの人は、新たな意識が産業の質をアップグレードするのだと信じています。

　では、アメリカに影響を与えたアジアはどうでしょうか。日本を例に取れば、第二次世界大戦を境に**徹底的に**欧米の民主主義のシステムを取り入れ、産業の**再生**に取り組みました。しかし、そうした制度を支える価値観を横に置いて、**表層的な**制度と仕組みだけを導入したことが、その後の日本社会に様々な**消化不良**を起こしました。

　一方、中国では長年にわたる社会の混乱の末に**共産主義政権**が誕生し、文化大革命を経験した後には資本主義**との妥協**を進め、GDPも著しく伸長しました。しかし、これらのプロセスは、多くのアジアの国々に共通した負の遺産をもたらしたようです。自国の産業育成を優先する中で、元々アジアにあった様々な価値観のプラスの部分が、ともすれば**置き捨てられた**のです。

　例えば、日本の場合、産業育成のための教育が優先され、教育の最も基本的な部分といえる**人間性の追求**が**後回し**にされ、組織に従順な人間が「優秀な」人間とされました。その結果、従来の日本人社会にあった「融通」「謙譲」「和」といった価値観までもが**希薄化してしまった**のです。

　もちろん、こうした伝統的な価値観には負の部分もあるでしょう。しかし、負の部分を切除したとき、プラスの部分までもが壊死しかけたのです。

　中国では、文化大革命を通してアジア的な価値観の核であった**儒教道徳**そのものが崩壊し、その後**拝金主義**によるモラルハザードが起こりました。しかも、国民がそ

第6章

society emerged where it was taboo for people to talk about such contradictions.

In this way, Asian moral values deteriorated due to "indigestion" caused by the rapid absorption of Western culture, resulting in a twisted society.

And in the West, as typified by Silicon Valley, a new phenomenon is taking root in which Asian culture flows onto the foundation of traditional Western values.

This is the **precursor** of a reversal of the magnetic field in the cultural history of humankind. Just as the reverse of the magnetic field **plunges humanity into crisis**, the deterioration of the magnetic field of civilization is creating a significant **distortion** in our society. The core of Asian values is shifting to the West, and the core of the original moral hazard of Western capitalism is shifting to Asia. The **rift** in the US-China relationship is nothing less than a conflict over morality between the US, which has absorbed Asian values and created a diverse society, and Asian countries, represented by China, which have rushed to modernize their industries and **standardize** their societies.

This conflict of consciousness is the challenge left to the next generation of humankind. Can the US overcome prejudice and discrimination as a reaction to **immigrant society** and grow further? How can China and Japan **rejuvenate** their societies by gathering the advantages of flexibility and ancient Asian values? As we look toward the future, we need to keep our eyes on these fundamental changes in human values.

んな矛盾を語ることをタブーとする**統制社会**までもが出
現しました。

　このように、アジアでは欧米の文化の急激な吸収によ
る消化不良から、従来の道徳的な価値観が劣化し、社会
にいびつなねじれが発生したのです。

　そして、欧米ではシリコンバレーに代表されるように、
欧米の伝統的な価値観の土台の上にアジアの文化が流れ
込むという、新たな現象が定着しつつあるのです。

　これが人類の文化史における磁場の逆転現象の**前兆**で
す。地球の磁場の逆転が**人類を危機に陥れる**ように、文
明の磁場が逆転することで、人類は社会に大きな歪みを
つくりつつあります。アジアの価値の核が欧米に、元々
あった欧米から資本主義のモラルハザードの核がアジア
に移動しているのです。米中関係の**亀裂**は、
アジアの価値などを吸収して多様性社会を
生み出したアメリカと、産業の近代化を急
ぎ社会を**画一化**しようとした中国に代表さ
れるアジア諸国とのモラルをめぐる対立に
他ならないのです。

　この意識の対立が次世代に残された人類の課題です。
アメリカが**移民社会**への反動としての偏見と差別を克服
して、さらに成長できるか。中国や日本がいかに柔軟性
とアジア古来の価値観の長所を集め、**潤いを取り戻せる**
か。未来に向けて、こうした人の価値観の根本的な変化
に目を向けてゆく必要があるのです。

第6章

Key word

VALUE 価値、価値観

　「善悪・好悪といった価値」やそれを判断する「ものの見方・基準」を指します。後者の意味の場合はvaluesという複数形で表されます。動詞として使われる場合は「重んじる、尊ぶ」という意味です。これまで本書で何度も解説されてきたように、世界には国や地域、文化ごとにさまざまな価値観があり、それは時代とともに変遷してゆくものでもあります。これから世界を生きてゆくために、まずは自分が何に価値を認めるのか自覚すること。そして、他者が何を重んじているのか、その価値観を認めること。そして、異なる価値観を対立させず互いに受け入れていくことが、私たちや次の世代に残された課題だといえるでしょう。

例文

Every value has its good and bad aspects.
どんな価値観にも良い面と悪い面がある。

It is difficult to relate to someone who has different values from you.
価値観の違う相手とうまくやっていくのは難しい。

Japanese society values punctuality.
日本社会は時間を守ることを大切にしている。

? あなたはどう答える？

What do you think are the advantages and disadvantages of both Western and Japanese values?
欧米の価値観と日本の価値観、双方の利点と欠点は何だと思いますか？

ヒント▶ これまでの記事に出てきた双方の価値観、例えばプロテスタンティズムや個を尊重する欧米、調和や受容を大切にする日本、お互いのプラスとマイナスを考えてみましょう。

覚えておくと便利な単語、表現

☐ **diversity awareness**　多様性の尊重
☐ **incorporate ~ into**　〜を…に取り入れる
☐ **put ~ in context of**　〜を…の文脈でとらえる

第29話
人種や宗教の対立を乗り越えるには

Article 29
Overcoming Racial and Religious Conflicts

Do you remember that feeling? It seemed as if the forces of progress were on the march, that they were inexorable. Each step he took, you felt this is the moment when the old structures of violence and repression and ancient hatreds that had so long stunted people's lives and confined the human spirit – that all that was crumbling before our eyes.

—— Barack Obama

（みなさん、あの感覚を覚えていますか。みんなで歩いて勝ち取った止めることのできない流れ。彼が成し遂げた一つ一つのこと。それによって人々を絶望させ、人々の精神を押さえ込んできた古来以来の憎悪や抑圧、暴力の構造が、我々の目の前で崩壊しはじめたと思ったことを）

Article 29

In late 2021, Desmond Mpilo Tutu, a longtime South African fighter against **racial segregation policies** and protester against the oppression of human rights for black people, died. He was 90 years old. Another person who fought against **apartheid** has passed away.

Three and a half years earlier, on July 17, 2018, in Johannesburg, South Africa, a ceremony to celebrate the 100th anniversary of the birth of Nelson Mandela, who, like Tutu, had dedicated his life to eliminating racial discrimination, was held.

Nelson Mandela was born in 1918. He devoted his life to eliminating apartheid and was detained and imprisoned for 27 years beginning in 1964 by the then government, whose motto was "**white supremacy**." His greatest achievement was to create a society that **reconciled** the previously dominant white population with the oppressed black population.

Generally, when a system is overthrown by a revolution or other means, racial and ethnic hatreds erupt, and bloodshed is expected as **retaliation**. When Mandela became leader, he rejected retaliation for the severe discrimination he had faced.

Former US President Barack Obama was invited to speak at the July 17 ceremony as a **guest of honor**. In his speech, he talked about how Gandhi did not resort to violence when he led the movement for independence from the British in India and how he devoted himself to resolving the conflict between Hindus and Muslims even after independence. He emphasized that Gandhi's ideas were passed on to Dr. Martin Luther King, Jr., who later led the movement to eliminate discrimination against blacks in the

▶ reconcile → p.270

　2021年の暮れに、南アフリカで長きにわたって**人種隔離政策**と闘い、黒人への人権抑圧に抗議してきたデズモンド・ムピロ・ツツ氏が死去しました。90歳でした。**アパルトヘイト**と闘った人がまた一人、この世を去りました。

　その3年半前の2018年7月17日、南アフリカのヨハネスブルグで、ツツ氏と同様に人種差別の撤廃に生涯を捧げた、ネルソン・マンデラ氏の生誕100周年を祝う式典がありました。

　ネルソン・マンデラ氏が生まれたのは1918年。彼はアパルトヘイトの撤廃に生涯を捧げ、1964年から27年間、**白人優越主義**をモットーにしていた当時の政府によって拘束され服役しました。彼の最大の功績は、それまで支配層であった白人系の人々と、抑圧されていた黒人系の人々とが**融和する**社会づくりを目指したことにあります。

　一般的に、支配されていた層の人々が革命などによって制度が転覆されたとき、そこには人種や民族の憎悪が吹き出し、**報復**による流血も予想されます。マンデラ氏は、自らが国家の指導者になったとき、本人をも見舞った厳しい差別への報復を否定したのです。

　7月17日の式典には、アメリカのオバマ元大統領が来賓として招かれ、講演を行いました。彼はその講演において、インドでイギリスからの独立運動をガンジーが指導したとき、暴力に訴えず、独立後もヒンドゥー教徒とイスラム教徒との対立解消に心血を注いだことを語りました。そして、ガンジーの思想がその後アメリカで黒人への差別撤廃運動を行なったキング牧師に、さらに2013年に他界したマンデラ氏へと受け継がれてきたことを強

▶アパルトヘイトはアフリカーンス語で「隔離」を意味する、南アフリカ共和国での人種隔離政策のこと。法律で人種を白人・アジア人・カラード・黒人の4つに分け、居住や公共施設の使用、結婚、教育などを区別した。

デズモンド・ムピロ・ツツ

第6章

US, and to Mandela, who passed away in 2013.

Obama then warned that such racial and ethnic reconciliation attempts can be **undermined** by irresponsible populism. The lecture was given in response to the Black Lives Matter movement that spread across the United States in 2020 in response to a series of **assaults** on blacks by white police officers.

On the other hand, in South Africa, after Mandela became president, society was shaken by **poverty** and crime among the black population, which had suffered from racial discrimination for many years. In neighboring Zimbabwe, which, like South Africa, had abolished white rule, retaliation by the ruling class against the white community has become an issue.

These **human trials** of racial, ethnic, and even religious conflicts have yet to be overcome. Since Gandhi's death, India has been divided from Pakistan, which has a large Muslim population, and the two countries remain **in a state of tension**.

Certainly, if society is shaken in this way, it will also cause rampant populism that easily criticizes it.

Nelson Mandela was released in 1990. It was the year after the **collapse of the Berlin Wall** and the beginning of the **dismantling** of the Cold War's structures. Looking back on that time, former President Barack Obama emphasized that he **felt firsthand** the strong swell of the world's desire to finally overcome racial divisions and come together as one. The man who symbolized the "strong tide of freedom" that swept the world in the late 1980s and 1990s, which Obama spoke of fondly, was Nelson Mandela.

The Iron Curtain is long gone, and Eastern Europe, where

調しました。

　その上でオバマ氏は、そうした人種や民族の融和への試みが、無責任なポピュリズムによって**踏みにじられ**ようとしていると警告します。それは、2020年に、アメリカで白人の警察官による黒人への**暴行**事件が相次ぎ、Black Lives Matterとよばれる人権擁護の運動が全米に広がったことを受けた講演でした。

　一方、マンデラ氏が大統領になった後の南アフリカでは、長年人種差別を受けてきた黒人層の**貧困**や犯罪で社会が大きく揺れています。また、南アフリカ同様に白人支配を撤廃してきた隣国ジンバブエでは、支配層による白人社会への報復が問題視されました。

　こうした人種や民族、さらには宗教の対立という**人類の試練**は、今なお克服されていないのです。ガンジー亡き後、インドはイスラム教徒が多く住むパキスタンと分断され、二つの国は今でも一触即発の**緊張関係にある**のです。

　確かに、このように社会が揺れれば、それを安易に批判するポピュリズムが横行する原因ともなるはずです。

　ネルソン・マンデラ氏が釈放されたのは1990年。それは、**ベルリンの壁が崩壊**し、冷戦構造が**瓦解**し始めた翌年のことでした。オバマ元大統領は当時を振り返り、いよいよ世界が人種の対立を乗り越えて、一つになろうとする強いうねりを**肌で感じた**ことを強調します。オバマ氏が懐かしげに語った80年代終盤から90年代にかけて世界を見舞った「自由を求める強い潮流」を象徴した人物が、ネルソン・マンデラだったのです。

　しかし、今になって鉄のカーテンがなくなり、民主主

第6章

democracy was supposed to have been introduced, is reeling from the Russian invasion of Ukraine. The wave of strong repression of **nationalist movements** in Russia after the collapse of the Soviet Union has become a strong swell that has brought about **hostility** toward Ukraine, which was already seeking to align itself with Western countries in Russia. This hostility is now threatening the world.

Many people around the world wonder if the strong current toward a brighter future in the early 1990s may have been just an illusion. In the Middle East, ISIS has spread fear worldwide, and refugees have **flooded into** Europe amid the chaos. In China, the confidence that comes with economic growth has been overshadowed by **rampant censorship of free speech**, and the government is dealing with the protests of ethnic minorities with great force. Then Russia invaded neighboring Ukraine, killing many of its citizens.

For those who had seen Mandela's reforms with glowing eyes, was such a past a **fleeting illusion**? The war between Russia and Ukraine may **drag on**. The longer the war continues, the more human rights violations will happen.

As the world is newly divided into East and West, and each nation is divided by economic disparities, we must find the wisdom to overcome this crisis for the sake of future generations.

義が導入されたはずの東ヨーロッパは、ウクライナへの
ロシアの侵攻で大きく揺れています。ソ連崩壊後のロシ
アでの**民族運動**への強い弾圧の波が、ロシアの中ですで
に欧米諸国との連携を求めていたウクライナへの**敵愾心**
をもたらす強いうねりとなり、世界に脅威を与えていま
す。

　今や世界の多くの人々は、90年代初頭に人々が感じた
未来に向けた強い流れは、単なる幻だったのではと思う
ようになりました。中東ではISISが恐怖を世界に撒き散
らし、混乱の中で難民がヨーロッパ**に押し寄せました。**中
国では経済成長による自信の陰で、**言論統制**がごく当然
のごとく**横行**し、政府は少数民族の抗議にも強権をもっ
て対処しています。そしてロシアが隣国ウクライナに侵
攻し、多くの市民が犠牲となっているのです。

　マンデラ氏の改革を、目を輝かせて見ていた人々にと
って、そんな過去は**一瞬の幻**だったのでしょうか。ロシ
アとウクライナの軍事衝突は**長引く**かもしれません。戦
闘が長引くだけ人権の蹂躙も続きます。
　世界が新たに東西に分断され、それぞれの国家の中も
経済的格差で分断されるなか、我々は次世代のためにも
こうした危機を乗り越える知恵を見出さなければならな
いのです。

第6章

Key word

RECONCILE 和解［調和］させる

　「対立（conflict）している人・考えを隔てなくさせる、仲裁する」ことを表す他動詞です。本文には名詞reconciliation（融和、調和）もでてきます。

　ツツ氏やマンデラ氏、キング牧師、そしてガンジーと、人種や民族、宗教などの対立解消に尽力した先人たちによって歴史は受け継がれてきました。しかし、21世紀の今に至るまで完全に克服されることのないまま、世界は新たな分断の歴史を歩みはじめています。彼らが描いた未来を実現するために、今を生きる私たちはこの分断を融和に向けていく方法を考えていかなければならないのです。

例文

He was finally reconciled with his friend.
彼はようやく友人と和解した。

She managed to reconcile her work with her family life.
彼女はどうにか仕事と家庭を両立させた。

The South African reconciliation showed great political courage.
南アフリカの融和は大きな政治的勇気を示した。

❓ あなたはどう答える？

What divisions have emerged in Japanese society?
日本社会にはどのような分断が生まれていますか？

ヒント　正規・非正規や地域による賃金の格差や派生して生じる教育の格差。アルゴリズムによる自分好みのネット世界で形成される極端な志向と不寛容。他に考えられることは？

覚えておくと便利な単語、表現

☐ **divide into**　〜に分かれる

☐ **equitable society**　平等な社会

☐ **overcome the division**　分断を克服する

エピローグ

世代を超えた人類の葛藤と闘いのその先へ

Epilogue

Beyond the Conflicts and Struggles of Mankind across Generations

最終話
犠牲を乗り越えた人類の長い道のり

Last Story
The Long Road to Humanity Overcoming Sacrifice

Shall I curse the hour when first I saw the light of day, would it not have been better a thousand times when I died when I was born. Would I want to explain but my tongue remains powerless for now do I clearly see to be spurned is my lot. But would it be my greatest joy to know that it is you I love, for to you do I vow and a promise I make its you alone for whom I would lay my life.

—— Leona Florentino

（私が最初に光を感じた時を呪うのか。生を受けた時に死を迎えた方がはるかによかったと。語りたくても、言葉が足りず、無力なまま、今私は私の定めに逆らえないことがはっきりとわかっていても。でも、私が愛したのはあなただけだとわかったことが、そしてあなた一人に私の命を捧げることを誓ったことが、至上の喜びだと、言えないのだろうか）

In 1849, a woman was born in the Philippines.

Leona Florentino was the daughter of a **notable** family in Vigan, an ancient capital, about a 12-hour journey north of Manila.

A Spanish colony ruled the Philippines at the time. Vigan still **retains the ambiance** of the colonial city, and the old town there has been listed as a UNESCO **World Heritage site**.

As a child, Leona was very active. It is recorded that she annoyed her parents by riding a horse, which was not allowed for women according to the customs of the time. She had a **natural talent** for words and wrote poetry in the local language from an early age. However, because Leona was a woman, she was not allowed to go to college. Instead, she received education in the Spanish language from her mother and a **priest** who noticed her talent. She translated and spelled out the poems she had created in the Ilocano language into Spanish. It is said that her records provide **valuable clues** to the culture of the Ilocos region at that time.

Catholic society in the 19th century, especially in **remote** Philippine towns, was strict in its customs. Leona was forced into marriage at the age of 14 and became the wife of an influential man.

However, her husband and children did not appreciate her **independent-minded** behavior. Finally, she developed tuberculosis, was **quarantined** in a separate house, and died at the age of 35. She was forbidden to see even her children, partly because people feared **contagion** with tuberculosis, but also because people in the area disliked the influence she had on others, and

1849年に一人の女性がフィリピンで生まれました。

彼女の名前はレオナ・フロレンティーノ。彼女はマニラから車ではるか12時間以上北に移動したところにある、ビガンという古都の**名士**の家の娘として育てられました。

当時、フィリピンはスペインの植民地でした。ビガンには今でも植民地時代の街の**面影が残り**、その旧市街は**世界遺産**にも登録されています。

ビガンの旧市街

彼女は子どもの頃から活発でした。当時の慣習で女性には許されない乗馬をするなど、親を困らせたという記録も残っています。彼女は言葉への**天性の才能**があり、幼い頃から現地の言葉で詩作をします。しかし、レオナは女性ということで、大学に進めませんでした。その代わり、母親や彼女の才能に気付いた**神父**からスペイン語の教育を受け、ビガンがあるイロコス地方の言葉で創作した詩をスペイン語に訳し、綴り続けました。その記録は、当時のイロコス地方の文化を知る上でも**貴重な手がかり**になるといわれています。

19世紀のカトリック社会、それもフィリピンの**辺境の**街のしきたりは厳しいものでした。彼女は14歳で結婚を強いられ、街の有力者の妻になります。

しかし、**自立心旺盛な**彼女の行動は夫や子どもたちにも疎まれました。そして、ついに結核を発症したことから別居の上**隔離**され、35歳でこの世を去ったのです。結核が**伝染**すること以上に、彼女の影響を受けることを嫌った周囲の人々によって、子どもと会うことも禁じられた**軟禁生活**の中での死でした。彼女の死後、その情熱的

エピローグ

she died **under house arrest**. After her death, her passionate poetry was introduced by one of her sons and eventually made its way to Europe and America. Just 22 poems were delivered to Madrid, but they then spread to other major cities worldwide.

Their content led some to speculate that she might have been lesbian. Neither her ideas nor her actions were accepted by the society of her time, and the flame of her life was extinguished.

However, she is considered a **pioneer** of feminism in the Philippines. On a global level, her existence seems to have been forgotten **with the passage of time**. Nevertheless, the flame that was lit in her heart was quietly passed on from generation to generation and eventually became a strong **bonfire**. The Philippines has had female presidents, like Corazon Aquino, while, for example, the human rights activist and journalist Maria Ressa became the first Filipino woman to win the Nobel Peace Prize. This was 137 years after Leona Florentino passed away.

That number is a testament to how much time and passion it takes for humanity to achieve a result.

The history of mankind is changing little by little while swaying left and right and back and forth. It takes hundreds of years to recognize these movements as progress. If we look at history that way, the **violations of human rights** that are happening now in Ukraine, Myanmar, and other parts of the world may be one page in the long story of the suffering of humankind. Moreover, the suffering of those who are actually **writhing** in the whirlpool of history is immeasurable. When Leona Florentino was writing poetry alone while coughing up blood, there was no one there who understood her, and even though her son

な詩は、一人の息子によって紹介され、やがてヨーロッパやアメリカにも伝わりました。たった22編の詩がマドリードに伝えられたのち、世界の主要都市に広がったのです。

　その詩の内容から、彼女は同性愛者ではなかったかと推測されます。彼女の意識も行動も当時の社会には受け入れられずに、命の炎を燃やし尽くしたのです。

　しかし今、彼女はフィリピンのフェミニズムの**先駆者**と見なされています。世界レベルで見るならば、彼女の存在は**時の流れと共に**忘れ去られてしまったようです。とはいえ、彼女の心の中に灯った炎は世代と共に静かに受け継がれ、やがてしっかりとした**かがり火**となりました。コラソン・アキノ氏のようにフィリピンにも女性の大統領が生まれ、例えば、フィリピンの人権活動家でジャーナリストのマリア・レッサ氏は、フィリピン人の女性として初のノーベル平和賞を受賞しました。それは、レオナ・フロレンティーノが他界して137年後のことでした。

コラソン・アキノ

　この年月は、人類が一つのことに結果を出すまでに、どれだけの時間と情熱が必要かということを物語っています。

　人類の歴史は左右前後に揺れながら、少しずつ変化しています。それを進歩として認識するには数百年の時の流れが必要です。歴史をそのように捉えれば、今ウクライナで、さらにはミャンマーや世界のあちこちで起きている**人権の蹂躙**も、人類の長い苦悩の中の1ページなのかもしれません。しかも、実際に歴史の渦の中で**悶えている**人の苦悩は計り知れません。レオナ・フロレンティーノが喀血しながら一人で詩作をしていたとき、そこには理解者は誰もおらず、たまたま彼女の息子が母の死後にその作品をまとめたとしても、彼女自身の**葛藤**と生き様

エピローグ

happened to compile her work after her death, he could not share her own **struggles** and way of life.

Her son, Isabelo de Los Reyes, who introduced her poems, later threw himself into the revolutionary movement in the Philippines and continued to work as a writer and journalist, despite being **imprisoned** due to Spanish repression. After the Philippines was ceded from Spain to the US, he continued to **fight for independence** and for workers' rights. He passed away in 1938, before the Philippines **won its sovereignty** after World War II.

When you think about the fact that Leona Florentino's thoughts were passed on to her son in a way she never expected, you can realize the unexpected impact of human beings' long history. Let us hope that such intergenerational **conflicts** and struggles will have the power to save and guide humanity.

Perhaps we should remind ourselves that the cries of her soul are also an extension of the tragedy in Ukraine and the unreasonable violations of human rights that are taking place worldwide.

► conflict → p.280

を共有することはできませんでした。

　彼女の詩を紹介した息子イサベロ・デ・ロ・レイズは、その後フィリピンの革命運動に身を投じ、スペインの弾圧を受けて**投獄され**ながらも、ライターとして、ジャーナリストとして活動を続けました。フィリピンがスペインからアメリカに譲渡された後も、**独立のために戦い**、労働者の権利のためにも奔走しました。彼が他界したのは第二次世界大戦後にフィリピンが**主権を勝ち取る**よりも前、1938年のことでした。

　レオナ・フロレンティーノの思いが、本人が予想もしないなかで息子に受け継がれたことを思うとき、人類の歴史の思わぬ結実を実感させられました。そんな世代を超えた**葛藤**と闘いが、人類を救い導く力であることを祈念したいものです。

　ウクライナでの悲劇、そして世界各地で起きている理不尽な人権の蹂躙の彼方に、彼女の魂の叫びもあるのだということを、我々は思い出さなければならないのかもしれません。

イサベロ・デ・ロ・レイズ

エピローグ

Key word

CONFLICT 対立、葛藤

「〔個人の内面や個人・集団の間で〕考え方などが対立・矛盾すること」やそれによる「苦しみ、緊張状態」を指します。そこから発生する「〔長期の〕争い、紛争、戦闘」も意味します。

かつてレオナ・フロレンティーノが強いられた女性としてのしきたりや、植民地支配の後遺症による南北問題など、今なお世界各地にはさまざまな対立や葛藤が生まれ、苦しめられている人たちがいます。そして、こうした歴史を変えるために闘った多くの人々の血や涙が流されてきていることも、私たちは知っておかなければなりません。

例文

Conflict is mental struggle resulting from incompatible or opposing needs, wishes, or external or internal demands.
葛藤とは相容れない、あるいは対立するニーズや希望、あるいは外的・内的要求から生じる精神的な苦悶のことだ。

The conflict between blacks and whites in the state became worse.
州内の黒人と白人の対立はさらにひどくなった。

This conflict plagues people all over the world.
この争いは世界中を悩ませている。

 あなたはどう答える？

Please describe someone who fought for something in Japan.
日本で何かのために闘った人について紹介してください。

 今日の私たちの生活や権利が保障されているのは、先人たちの尽力の賜物に他なりません。あなたの知っている人や尊敬する人、誰かの物語を英語で伝えてみましょう。

覚えておくと便利な単語、表現

☐ **continue to fight for** 〜のために闘い続ける
☐ **pass on from generation to generation** 世代を超えて伝える
☐ **result of hard work** 努力の結晶

English Conversational Ability Test
国際英語会話能力検定

● E-CATとは…
英語が話せるようになるための
テストです。インターネットベ
ースで、30分であなたの発話力
をチェックします。

● iTEP®とは…
世界各国の企業、政府機関、アメリカの大学300
校以上が、英語能力判定テストとして採用。オン
ラインによる90分のテストで文法、リーディン
グ、リスニング、ライティング、スピーキングの
5技能をスコア化。iTEP®は、留学、就職、海外
赴任などに必要な、世界に通用する英語力を総
合的に評価する画期的なテストです。

www.ecatexam.com

www.itepexamjapan.com

日英対訳
英語で話す世界情勢

2023年 3 月 1 日　第 1 刷発行
2024年 1 月 16 日　第 2 刷発行

著　者　　山久瀬洋二

発行者　　浦　晋亮

発行所　　IBCパブリッシング株式会社
　　　　　〒162-0804 東京都新宿区中里町 29 番 3 号 菱秀神楽坂ビル
　　　　　Tel. 03-3513-4511　Fax. 03-3513-4512
　　　　　www.ibcpub.co.jp

印刷所　　株式会社シナノパブリッシングプレス

ISBN978-4-7946-0751-5